"*Corporate Catalysts* is a very practical guide to honing leadership skills. It will stimulate a thorough self-evaluation and help you do the best you are capable of doing."

Michael Hurst, President/COO,
McCarthy Building Companies, Inc.

"*Corporate Catalysts* describes in easily understood terms how employees at every level in an organization can become highly influential 'catalysts' and produce superior results. That's a major task, but one Coughlin accomplishes by providing common sense steps for needed actions and methodologies to use for success."

Debbie Lewis, Vice President,
Human Resources, T Mobile USA

"*Corporate Catalysts* is a must read for new and veteran managers alike. It focuses on methodologies to generate significant, sustainable, and profitable growth as a result of focusing on highest priority business outcomes. Dan Coughlin's mantra to focus on the long term and execute in the short term resonates with the experienced business professional."

Michael T. Wijas, National Sales Director,
Boston Scientific Corporation

"When it comes to business coaching, Dan Coughlin is the best! *Corporate Catalysts* is a great blueprint for success for any person in business, regardless of the industry. This will be a 'must read' for all of my executives."

Joseph L. Uhl, Area General Manager, Marriott International

"Dan Coughlin brings a variety of useful tools that are targeted at desired business results. He then works with you to shape these into processes that will focus your work on your desired business outcomes. The benefit is that as your people grow and progress, they take these learnings with them and, most importantly, leave behind the process that will benefit others."

Lee Renz, Vice President/General Manager,
McDonald's Corporation

"Dan Coughlin continues to push the edge for me to be a better leader and to make my organization more effective."

Mike Slocum, Senior Director, The Coca-Cola Company

"I found it easy to apply Dan Coughlin's concepts in *Corporate Catalysts* to parallels within my own organization. Each chapter encouraged me to maintain successful leadership."

Lorri Keenum, CEO/President,
Midwest Trenching & Excavating, Inc.

"I have talked to numerous customers regarding *Corporate Catalysts*, and at great length with my peers. Comments in the book like, 'Don't just stop the orchestra to hear myself talk,' and, 'Create an environment where motivated people succeed' mean a lot in today's business environment. *Corporate Catalysts* is now the book I recommend to business associates and clients."

Ken Placke, Business Manager, Frank Leta Acura

"I really enjoyed *Corporate Catalysts*. While many authors have explained the art of leadership, Dan Coughlin's refreshing perspective sheds more light on this topic and explains it better than most. This book makes a real contribution to the discussion of change makers and clarifiers."

Eugene Mackey, Principal, Mackey Mitchell Associates

"*Corporate Catalysts* outlines a practical, no nonsense approach on how anyone, regardless of where they are in the organization, can step up to be a more effective manager and leader. It is jam-packed with pearls of wisdom that provide great insight on how a manager can improve their value and contribution to the organization they support. The book is easy to read and complete with practical and interesting stories that complement the presented ideas on becoming a corporate catalyst."

Mike Yonker, Regional Vice President, Human Resources,
Marriott International

"*Corporate Catalysts* has great practical steps to mold a more effective and influential leader. Since Dan Coughlin has been my Executive Coach for the past few years, I have acted upon many of the recommendations in this book such as the subtle management tips and tools of influence that have yielded great results."

Karen Wells, Vice President/General Manager,
McDonald's Corporation

CORPORATE CATALYSTS

How to Make Your Company
More Successful,
Whatever Your Title, Income, or Authority

Dick, 1/3/05

Thank you for your
friendship & support!

Dan Coughlin

DAN COUGHLIN

CAREER
PRESS

Franklin Lakes, NJ

CORPORATE CATALYSTS
EDITED AND TYPESET BY KRISTEN PARKES
Cover design by DesignConcept
Printed in the U.S.A. by Book-mart Press

To order this title, please call toll-free 1-800-CAREER-1 (NJ and Canada: 201-848-0310) to order using VISA or MasterCard, or for further information on books from Career Press.

The Career Press, Inc., 3 Tice Road, PO Box 687,
Franklin Lakes, NJ 07417
www.careerpress.com

Library of Congress Cataloging-in-Publication Data

Coughlin, Dan, 1962-
    Corporate catalysts : how to make your company more successful, whatever your title, income, or authority / by Dan Coughlin.
        p. cm.
    Includes index.
    ISBN 1-56414-781-9 (paper)
        1. Organizational effectiveness. 2. Industrial management. I. Title.

HD58.9.C675 2005
658.4'01--dc22

2004057006

To Barb, Mom, Dad, Hutch, and Alan,
the five people who've made my work possible.

ACKNOWLEDGMENTS

To all of my clients at McDonald's Corporation, Marriott International, The Coca-Cola Company, Citigroup, the St. Louis Cardinals, GSD&M, SBC Communications, McCarthy Building Companies, Fru-Con Construction, Heartland Dental Care, Successories, Eli Lilly, Brown Shoe Company, American Bar Association, Four Seasons Group, Cassens Transport, Midwest Trenching & Excavating, Ritter's Frozen Custard, ANDEO Nalco Chemical, and other organizations. You taught me far more than I taught you. Thank you all very much.

Special recognition to two very special clients: Lee Renz and Karen Wells. They are true corporate catalysts. Without Lee Renz, this book would never have been written. You taught me the most. Karen Wells has been a true business partner and has taught me a great deal.

Thanks to Jeff Hutchison, one of my biggest supporters and greatest friends for the past 25 years. Thanks to Alan Weiss, my extraordinary mentor, who pushed me to write this book. Thanks to Mike Feder for 15 years of sharing and realizing dreams. Thanks to Jerry Yeagley and Ted Drewes, who taught me how to be an entrepreneur. Thanks to Tom Becvar, who taught me how to teach effectively and passionately. Thanks to my MBA students in Managerial Leadership at Webster University. This book is based in part on our work together. Thanks to the two iconic organizations that affected my life the most: St. Louis University High School and the University of Notre Dame. They provided a large part of my ongoing foundation.

Thanks to Jeff Herman, my literary agent, and the whole team at Career Press, who believed in this concept and opened a great new door for me. I truly appreciate everything you have done.

Special thanks to my wonderful wife, Barb, and our two children, Sarah and Ben, for supporting me and believing in me. I love you more than you'll ever know. Finally, thanks to my phenomenal parents, Gene and Laura Coughlin, who have served as the great catalysts in my life.

CONTENTS

INTRODUCTION

IN DECEMBER OF MY SENIOR YEAR IN COLLEGE, I decided to pursue a career as a head coach for college soccer. My degree was in engineering, but my calling was to work directly with people to achieve their desired outcomes. I thought sports would be the most obvious outlet. After I accepted the position as head soccer coach at Tri-State University, a small school in northeast Indiana, I started to meet regularly with my former coach, Dennis Grace, who at the time was the head soccer coach at the University of Notre Dame. One session in particular stands out in my mind. He said, "A truly great coach can take his and beat yours and then take yours and beat his." I knew what he meant instantly, but I didn't understand what he meant for many years. He was talking about "the catalyst," the person who raises the bar for any organization he or she joins.

This book is for people who want to play the role of the catalyst in an organization. These individuals want to cut through the corporate cacophony and be part of the solution, not the problem. They want to influence others to think differently and generate unexpected and improbable results. They want to be corporate catalysts. Many times these individuals operate behind the scenes and don't get the glory their less productive counterparts receive, and that's okay with them. They understand that the key to gaining respect is earning it.

Corporate catalysts don't see corporations as sleazy places where they have to act unethically in order to succeed. Instead, they view corporations as places to do meaningful work and make an extraordinary difference for their customers and fellow employees. Other people perceive them as the most valuable employees in their organizations.

Corporate catalysts are tremendous influencers and effective managers. They produce results in their organization's most important business outcomes through boring consistency and constant innovation, through common sense and strong character, and through building relationships while avoiding corporate fallacies. Along the way, they strengthen their income security, gain leadership of important projects, become more coveted by their employers and the competition, and attract better career opportunities.

After spending 10 years as a college and high school soccer coach, my career shifted to presenting workshops on leadership, management, teamwork, strategy, branding, and innovation to businesspeople all across the United States. One day a senior director at a large corporation said to me, "Dan, I want to work with you, but not in a classroom setting. I want to meet with you regularly and integrate you into my daily activities so you can help me be a more effective leader and manager in my actual business settings." Little did I know how that moment would permanently change my professional life. I attended his meetings, observed him in action, and discussed with him how he could more effectively achieve the desired business outcomes.

That relationship led to dozens more. I have provided more than 900 executive coaching sessions and more than 400 presentations to executives at McDonald's, Coca-Cola, Marriott, Citigroup, SBC Communications, Eli Lilly, the St. Louis Cardinals, IKON Office Solutions, Heartland Dental Care, Auxeris Therapeutics, McCarthy Construction, Fru-Con Construction, Brown Shoe Company, Successories, Cassens Transport, ANDEO Nalco Chemical, GSD&M, the American Bar Association, and many others. I invested more than 2,500 hours on-site with executives in private meetings, small group sessions, and large conferences in more than 20 industries. I worked with them to deal effectively with real-life business issues and accelerate the achievement of their most important desired business outcomes. In essence, the goal was for them to become corporate catalysts. Oftentimes, I learned more from them than they did from me.

Back in college, I knew Coach Grace meant that great coaches create winning teams even if they have a little less talent to work with than the other coaches. However, it took me nearly 20 years to understand how a catalyst creates a winning team in a corporation. This book summarizes my findings on how to accelerate your organization's critical business outcomes in a pragmatic way, regardless of your title, income, or authority. My hope is that you will be the catalyst in your organization and generate the unexpected results, even the improbable ones.

PART

The
Overview

Chapter 1

THE FALLACY OF EARNINGS PER SHARE

MANAGERS MAKE A COMMON MISTAKE when they repeatedly base their decisions on a false premise. A business premise called "Earnings per Share" (EPS) gained momentum in the mid-1980s and ultimately had an enormously adverse effect on corporations. This concept led companies on short-term wild-goose chases that ended up hurting their businesses far more than helping them. Here is a brief history of EPS, how it hurt the sustainable results of many organizations, and how it might be keeping you from making your company more successful over the long term.

The Evolution of the EPS Fallacy

Beginning in the 1980s, many executives said the purpose of a business is to increase shareholder wealth. Investors decided the best way to determine if shareholders were actually winning was to see whether or not the company's earnings per share (EPS) increased. If a company increased short-term earnings, investors assumed the company was growing more successful and more valuable. If quarterly earnings went up, the stock price went up. Then investors decided it wasn't enough to merely increase earnings. Corporations also had to increase revenue to prove their growth and to show they didn't just maximize their earnings per share. Finally, investors decided that if a company could demonstrate the potential to dramatically grow their revenue and earnings, they would assume the company would eventually be successful. Therefore, their stock went up again.

Just to make sure their executives stayed focused on increasing earnings per share and revenue, corporations decided to stop paying their senior executives large base salaries. Instead, they were paid with stock options. This way, the executives only made big money if their organizations "performed well" in terms of increasing short-term earnings and revenue, or they at least showed the capacity to dramatically increase earnings and revenue in the future.

That made sense for a time, but it turned out to be a terrible thought process. People with the EPS mentality believe the value of a company is equal to its growth in earnings per share during any given quarter. Far too many people passed over one very important word: the *perceived* value of the company. Companies really weren't better because they earned more in a given quarter, they only appeared to be better, and a lot of people bought into that misperception.

Once executives realized investors believed companies with high short-term revenue and earnings would definitely succeed over the long term, their behavior shifted from trying to run great companies to maximizing their short-term earnings and revenue. That simple shift in behavior caused some corporations to destroy billions of dollars of shareholder wealth, some businesses to collapse altogether, and far too many CEOs to be paid an exponential version of a king's ransom. Executives boosted short-term earnings and revenue, or rather the *perception* they could dramatically grow future earnings and revenue, in a variety of ways that hurt their businesses.

8 Non-sustainable Ways to Improve Earnings and Revenue

1.   Create instant growth through mergers and acquisitions.

From 1990 to 2000 we saw ever-increasing acquisitions and mergers run into the billions of dollars, even though, by some estimates,

40 percent of all businesses were worse off after the acquisition or merger than beforehand. In my community alone, one bank went from Boatmen's to NationsBank to Bank of America in approximately 18 months. The only people guaranteed to improve their situation were the sign-makers. AOL Time Warner became the ultimate poster child for how corporations consume themselves by increasing their revenue without creating additional value for customers.

2. Jump on bandwagons during economic boom times.

The dot-com phenomenon was the starkest example of the "Bandwagon Approach." Businesses didn't even have to operate in order to be declared valuable. Placing ".com" on the name of a business designated real value to far too many investors. However, even after the dot-com bubble burst in March 2000, executives still had not learned the lesson that you can only sell potential for so long. Business bandwagons do not generate sustainable, profitable growth. Once investors realize what they're dealing with, they run away faster than they jumped on board.

3. Reduce costs instantly.

In the name of increasing earnings per share, corporations sold off assets and withheld payments to suppliers as long as possible. These corporations focused far more on improving shareholder wealth than on improving their businesses.

4. Sell sex.

Unless you're running Playboy, Inc., using sexy women in your marketing efforts is not a sustainable approach to improving revenue and profits. Yet every major television network stepped away from developing quality stories and programming to overdosing the public with reality television shows. This did generate a spike in short-term revenue, but it did not create sustainable success. It's pretty hard to keep the public watching reruns of *The Bachelor* when they already know whom he selected as his wife.

5. Lie and cheat.

At the turn of the century, companies such as Enron, Arthur Andersen, WorldCom, Adelphia, and Parmalat boosted their short-term stock price by lying about their actual performance. A mania for getting instant results had so enraptured corporations that seemingly no deed was considered too outlandish to "prove" a company was doing well. James Brown, the former VP of finance for Adelphia Communications, admitted in court in May of 2004 that he and other officers basically just made up a variety of financial numbers to appease the analysts.

6. Be like GE.

Other companies chose to step far out of their core businesses and constantly diversify in order to maintain their revenue momentum. This concept worked at GE because of the depth of their management pool. Jacques Nasser, former CEO of Ford Motor Company, obsessed so much over becoming the next Jack Welch and creating the next GE that he eventually consumed his own career and nearly diversified an American icon into irreversible negative growth.

7. Pay me now and I'll pay my bills much, much later.

Another trick of the trade to boost short-term profits and revenues was to accept a multiple-year contract and count all of it as revenue in the first year. That way it appeared profits had risen extraordinarily for one year. Of course, there was the small problem of having no revenue from the project for the ensuing years while the costs for delivering the project came to fruition. But the attitude at the time was, "So what? We'll make today look great and worry about next year when it comes."

8. Just get rid of people.

When all else failed, corporations fired employees in record numbers. They argued that they couldn't afford to keep their employees and keep their commitments to their shareholders. Immediately after September 11, 2001, American Airlines announced they would lay off thousands of workers.

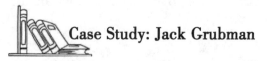 **Case Study: Jack Grubman**

Every crisis has real-life stories behind it. Perhaps no person represents the *fallacy of EPS* better than Jack Grubman. In his heyday, Jack Grubman served as a telecom analyst for Salomon Smith Barney, where he earned $20 million a year. In the November 18, 2001, issue of the *New York Times*, Gretchen Morgenson wrote:

> Since 1997, Salomon has taken in more investment banking fees from telecom companies than any other firm on the Street. Because of Mr. Grubman's power and prominence, and because his compensation is based in part on fees the company generated with his help, a part of those fees went to him. As he rallied clients of Salomon Smith Barney to buy shares of untested telecommunications companies and to hold on to the shares as they lost almost all their value, he was aggressively helping his firm win lucrative stock and bond deals from these same companies.

That's a classic example of the problem. Investors grew to trust that analysts would actually analyze a company and determine whether the company would truly be successful over the long term. Not only did many analysts succumb to the fallacy that high short-term earnings equaled long-term success, some even took it one step further: they created "value" for their clients by simply saying their businesses would succeed over the long term. This worked as long as the companies "demonstrated" high performance. Jack Grubman, for example, touted WorldCom as a highly successful company. Of course, we all know now that WorldCom made up its numbers, but we didn't realize back then what levels of greed were manifested by the fallacy of earnings per share. Once again, the mythological relationship between short-term earnings and the sustainable success of a company was bared for all to see.

My point is that focusing on increasing short-term revenues and/ or earnings in order to protect your stock price does not make a corporation more successful or valuable in the long term. In fact, it may ultimately do just the opposite.

EPS vs. SSPG

If focusing solely on improving short-term EPS isn't the answer, then what is it? Here's an acronym I like even better: SSPG. It stands for Significant, Sustainable, and Profitable Growth. Companies focused on SSPG realize the key to their success begins with understanding their desired customers' wants and needs. They work relentlessly to add more value to those customers by innovating within their core business, and brand their efforts by letting people know the value they actually deliver. This process takes time. It does not generate massive stock increases overnight. However, by sticking to this formula over the long term, companies can create incredible shareholder wealth.

Author's Note: Throughout this book I share insights from a variety of authors and executives who have influenced my thinking about corporate catalysts under the headings "Faculty Input From 'Corporate Catalysts University.'"

Faculty Input From "Corporate Catalysts University"

In 1992, shortly before he died, Sam Walton wrote 10 rules he used to grow Wal-Mart (*Sam Walton: Made in America*, Dell Publishing, 1992). Here are two of *Sam's Rules for Building a Business*:

Rule 1: Commit to your business.

Rule 8: Exceed your customers' expectations. If you do, they'll come back over and over.

In his book, Sam Walton explains repeatedly how to create sustainable and profitable growth. He teaches that SSPG begins with focusing on what the customer wants and needs, and constantly finding ways to add more value to those needs within the core purpose of your business.

The Relationship Between Corporate Catalysts and Long-Term Organizational Success

What does this have to do with being a corporate catalyst?

I started this book with a macro view of corporations and what approaches do and do not work, in order to make this point about individual employees: *If you want to serve as a corporate catalyst and accelerate your organization to SSPG, you MUST take the long-term view as you move into action every day.* Some employees try to gain attention by immediately impacting one spectacular outcome. If you fall in this category, beware of the danger of short-term thinking. Just as corporations rise and fall through their obsession with immediate successes, you also could be a fast riser on the way to a fast fall.

To improve the short-term in a sustainable way, you need to focus on the long term, and execute your approach every day. At first, this statement might not make sense because I just presented the argument that the fastest rising companies achieved unbelievable short-term results by focusing on short-term profits and revenues (for example, Enron, WorldCom, and HealthSouth). However, I said, "…improve the short-term in a *sustainable* way…." If you improve your business, and you continue to improve it over and over again, you will eventually have an extraordinary business. However, if you improve your revenues without improving your business, you build results on a house of cards. It's like the student who gets an A on the first test, but never develops the habits of a successful student. Not paying attention in class, not taking notes, not studying for tests, and not asking questions eventually catches up with him or her.

Corporate Catalysts Tip #1:
Connecting Today's Activities With
Tomorrow's Results
The person who keeps a group of people focused on the long term and executing in the short term is the group's most valuable player.

---

10 Ways to Focus Long Term and Execute Short Term

1. Define the purpose of the business.

Work to understand the business you're in. Keep talking with other people in your organization and your customers until you clearly understand the purpose of your business. Work at this until you can explain the purpose of your business in a sentence or two. Then make sure everyone in your group clearly understands the purpose of your business. Here are a few famous examples:

McDonald's is in the business of providing an extraordinary quick-service restaurant experience.

Southwest Airlines is in the business of democratizing air travel by providing cheap, fun, and convenient transportation.

2. Focus your meetings on business outcomes.

Begin every meeting by clarifying the specific business outcome your group is working to improve. Make sure the desired outcome fits within the framework of your core purpose as a business. When you clarify your group's HPOs (Highest Priority Business Outcomes), you take an important step toward accelerating SSPG. HPOs need to be outcomes, and not activities or internal milestones.

3. Walk your talk.

Have a list of your organization's "corporate values" with you at all times. When a discussion begins to gain momentum that could lead to behaviors not consistent with the stated values, ask, "If we were to do that, how would it be consistent with these values?" Bring this up early, before the train leaves the station.

4. Focus on customer victories.

When your group discusses a potential new activity, ask, "Which customer will benefit if we do that, and how will they be better off?" If a case can't be made that a customer will benefit, then don't do it. This eliminates a huge percentage of time-wasting activities.

5. Push back your boss.

When your boss wants to add a new activity to your plate, ask how it fits with the company's strategic direction. Don't say no, but also don't add it until you have an understanding of why it makes sense. Remain calm and patient even as your boss becomes impatient. Don't jump to add new activities that only have a short-term return on your investment.

6. Search to add more real value.

Ask the group to answer two questions: "In general, how do we add value to customers?" and "Within that approach, what else can we do to add more value to our customers?" For example, as I facilitated a planning session for one retail client, the participants decided the number-one item their customers wanted was faster service. They innovated with an emphasis on speed, and 18 months later, received rave reviews from a local business editor who tried to find fault in the faster service they promised.

7. Stick to your core business.

When an idea does not fit your company's core business, push back. Say, "Did you ever wonder why Southwest Airlines doesn't sell cappuccino while customers stand in line? It's because they focus on speed and keeping their ticket prices as low as possible. Serving cappuccino would slow things down and make the trip more expensive. We also have to stick with who we are as a business."

8. Avoid fads.

Right-sizing was a fad. TQM was a fad. Reengineering was a fad. They were all so-called "silver bullets" to remedy problems that masked much deeper problems. Understand the purpose of your business, know what your customers need, and keep delivering better value to them within the boundary of your business's purpose. That's the "silver bullet."

Leave the Little Stuff Alone

Ask yourself this question: "Is this a battle worth fighting, or should I save my energy for an issue that will have a greater impact on achieving our highest priority business outcomes?" If you take on every situation as though it will make or break your business, you won't be taken seriously.

9. Meet the emotional needs of other people.

Explain your rationale in terms of the emotional best interests of the other person. Say to a fellow employee, "You have two teenagers, is that right? You want to be part of a business that will be around when your children go to college, right? If we do something now that only has a six-month shelf life, and then we have to start all over again with a new idea, will we really be around to get your kids through college? Why not focus on ideas that are sustainable and can build on each other?"

10. Shift from internal issues to external focus.

When a turf war pops up between departments, pull the department heads together for lunch and ask, "What specific customer outcome are we trying to improve?" This way, you move the conversation toward a mutually objective discussion on how to better meet the customers' needs and away from who said what. Remember the "90/10 Rule," which I first learned from Dr. Alan Weiss, author of *Million-Dollar Consulting* (McGraw-Hill, 1992). It says the best companies in the world focus 90 percent of their resources on improving the client's condition and 10 percent of their resources on dealing with internal issues.

Author's Note: Each chapter ends with a section called "The Corporate Catalystic Converter," which provides suggestions on how to convert the ideas in that chapter into a working reality in your daily business activities.

THE CORPORATE CATALYSTIC CONVERTER

☑ The value of long-term thinking and the downside of short-term thinking.

"The Fallacy of Earnings per Share" is synonymous with "The Downside of Short-Term Thinking." It's not that having high earnings or short-term good results is a bad thing. The problem occurs if you only focus on improving short-term results and ignore building long-term, sustainable success.

☑ Define your business.

Work to clarify the purpose of your business. It has to be so clear that you can explain it conversationally. Without a clear understanding of the purpose of your business, there is no way to generate significant, sustainable, and profitable growth.

☑ Know your HPOs (Highest Priority Business Outcomes)

Write down your organization's three highest priority business outcomes. These are not activities. These are specific outcomes for the organization to achieve. Work with your boss, peers, direct reports, and staff members to clarify the three most important outcomes. You can't provide effective management and leadership unless you know the most important desired business outcomes for your organization.

☑ Clarify your strategic approach.

Discuss with your boss, peers, and staff members the specific approach your organization wants to take to deliver better value to your customers in order to achieve the desired results. Keep discussing the strategy until everyone understands it and can easily explain it.

☑ Analyze your activities.

Look at each of your group's activities and answer these two questions:

1. Does this activity have a significant impact on achieving one or more of our HPOs?
2. Does this activity fit within our strategic approach?

If you get a no to either question, try to stop doing that activity.

☑ Make necessary adjustments.

Ask the members of your group: "Are we maintaining a long-term view toward adding more value to our customers and building a meaningful brand, or are we focused solely on improving short-term profits and revenue?" If you find your activities do not generate sustainable results, shift toward tactics that provide a longer-term impact.

Recommended Resources for Corporate Catalysts

Sam Walton: Made in America by Sam Walton with John Huey (Dell Publishing, 1992).

This is the real-life story of one of the greatest CEOs of all time and told from his perspective. He maintained a simple business philosophy and focused on executing it every day.

Process Consulting by Alan Weiss (Jossey-Bass/Pfeiffer, 2002).

A true expert on organizational acceleration, Dr. Alan Weiss provides an array of tools for improving significant, sustainable, and profitable growth.

Chapter 2

PORTRAIT OF A CORPORATE CATALYST

A FEW YEARS AGO, I taught a course on managerial leadership for the Graduate School of Business at Webster University. During the third class session it finally dawned on me that a managerial leader is the most valuable employee because he or she is the organizational accelerator, the person who raises the performance bar for the whole company. Of course, "organizational accelerator" is a mouthful, so I reworked the idea and came up with "corporate catalyst."

A corporate catalyst serves as both a highly effective leader and a highly effective manager. One skill set applied without the other is insufficient. Leadership means influencing how other people think in a way that generates better sustainable results for your organization and the individuals in it. Management means converting the collective resources into better results. In Figure 2.1, notice the relationship between the two skill sets and how important both aspects are to accelerating your organization's critical business outcomes.

The Making of a Corporate Catalyst

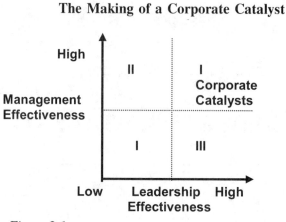

Figure 2.1

Quadrant I—This employee is poor as both a manager and a leader. He or she has no clear idea how to optimize available resources, hire the right people, or influence people toward more effective behaviors. At best, this person serves as an hourly worker doing exactly what his or her supervisor says to do. At worst, this type of employee acts as an enormous drain on corporate resources by keeping jobs he or she can't fulfill.

Quadrant II—This employee clarifies and communicates a framework for leveraging resources toward improved results, but is unable to influence other people to change their behaviors. On paper, the plan looks terrific, but it never gets converted into reality.

Quadrant III—This employee effectively influences people to consider new ideas and new behaviors. Unfortunately, this person provides no clear framework for how to convert new behaviors into sustainable results. He or she stimulates people to reach toward new heights, but provides no process for getting there.

Quadrant IV—This employee is the corporate catalyst. He or she understands the desired results, clarifies the key values for long-term success and the strategy for getting there, hires the right people, and constantly finds ways to improve the value the organization delivers to customers. In addition, he or she effectively influences people at various levels in the organization in a way that accelerates the desired results. In other words, this person masters the science of management and the art of leadership.

The Science of Management (Chapters 4, 5, and 7)

Effective managers do very similar things, including:

➢ **Define the *Playing Field* (Chapter 4).**

They work with the members of their group to clarify the Playing Field, shown in Figure 2.2, which includes the expected values, expected strategy, short-term results, and long-term results.

The Playing Field

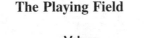

Figure 2.2

➢ **Hire the right people, fire the wrong people (Chapter 7).**

As Jim Collins wrote in *Good to Great* (HarperCollins, 2001), the manager's most important job is to get the right people on the bus and put them in the right seats, and get the wrong people off the bus.

➢ **Provide freedom within the framework (Chapter 4).**

Effective managers give members of their groups the room to make their own decisions on how to operate within the Playing Field. They get out of the way so the group members can think for themselves.

➢ **Hold people accountable (Chapter 4).**

They apply positive or negative consequences depending on whether their employees operate on or off the Playing Field.

➢ **Coach every individual (Chapter 4).**

They add value to each person by asking relevant, practical, and open-ended questions. They clarify the action plan and consistently follow up to make sure the members of their group stay on track.

➤ **Build a brand (Chapter 5).**

Effective managers make sure the efforts of their group resonate with customers and prospects in a meaningful way.

➤ **Stimulate innovation (Chapter 5).**

They regularly pull their team back from tactical execution and discuss ways to raise the bar in terms of adding more value to customers within the defined purpose of their business.

The Art of Leadership (Chapters 3, 6, 8, and 9)

While managers do predictable things, leaders influence people in widely differing ways. Leadership is less about approach and more about the shift in perspective of the other person. When a person's perspective changes, his or her attitudes, actions, and habits change as well. Great leaders are not tied to a particular personality type, title, income, or authority level. They differentiate themselves as leaders through their ability to affect other people's perspectives and behaviors in ways that lead to better results. They slice through the gray noise of myths, rumors, and misguided fallacies and maintain the group's focus on the few things that have the greatest positive impact on driving their critical business outcomes. Along the way, they create highly effective teams where each member supports every other member toward achieving a common objective.

What Does It Take to Be a Corporate Catalyst?

Corporate catalysts courageously do what they believe is the right thing to do, say what they see as the truth, and risk failure. Winston Churchill said, "Success is not final. Failure is not fatal. It is the courage to continue that counts." He was a great catalyst for Britain in World War II, and his philosophy applies to this day.

Corporate catalysts communicate clearly, which allows them to effectively influence all types of decision-makers in different situations. They impact people in private conversations, through participating in small group meetings and by speaking to large audiences. One vice president I worked with could give a 90-minute speech to a large audience, facilitate a small group discussion, and advise an individual on his or her next career move all before lunch. He understood influencing others is an art, not a science, and he always kept searching for subtle ways to make an even greater impact.

Corporate catalysts understand the big picture of the desired results, the framework for achieving those results, and the detailed work necessary to succeed. They get things done. Not content with merely telling others what to do, they work collaboratively with other people to determine the best approach for turning the plans into results. They are not afraid to step in and do some of the hands-on work, make the calls, go on-site with the front-line workforce, and tell the top executives in a professional manner where they made mistakes.

Corporate catalysts make tough decisions about people in order to get the right kind of people in the group and the wrong kind of people out of it. They take the time necessary to determine what type of person is needed in a given role and search until they find that person.

At all times, corporate catalysts maintain their sense of humor. They're like Joe Montana, the former quarterback of the San Francisco 49ers, in that classic story where he spotted the actor John Candy in the stadium during a timeout on the final come-from-behind drive in the Super Bowl. He turned to his teammates in the huddle, smiled, and calmly pointed out where Candy was sitting. Everyone relaxed and performed better under the enormous pressure.

Corporate Catalyst Tip #2:
The Value of Self-Assessment

Analyze your current strengths as a leader and as a manager. Step back from constant activities and analyze what you do well, what you don't do well, and what you could do better. Ask others for input. Have an objective third party conduct interviews with the people around you in your organization and your customers. Get feedback from them about what makes you effective and ineffective. Identify a few key areas to focus on and move back into action. With each step forward, you move toward being a corporate catalyst.

More than anything, corporate catalysts rely on common sense to guide their decisions. They don't get caught up in widely held business myths, but instead focus on doing what needs to be done to make their organization better. They don't play favorites, say what the group of the moment wants them to say, or become arrogant, no matter how brightly their star shines at any given moment.

Why Is It So Hard to Be a Corporate Catalyst?

Understanding what it means to be a corporate catalyst, why it's so important to become one, and how to become one seems very logical. So why don't more employees perform this incredibly valuable role in their organizations? The reason is because being a corporate catalyst is really very hard work. Challenges to becoming a corporate catalyst are discussed in the following sections.

Hidden Forces Beyond Your Control

The stock markets drops dramatically, your children get sick, business travel evaporates, your aging parents need greater attention, a key supplier goes out of business, a higher-level executive changes the strategic direction of your company, a computer virus attacks your key files, a catastrophic event happens in your industry, horrendous weather disintegrates sales, and on and on. You deal with critical variables for success that reside completely outside your control. This potential drop in results due to no fault of your own can frustrate you to the point of giving up. However, corporate catalysts accept these outside forces as part of the game. Instead of getting frustrated, they focus on the situations and people they can influence to move past the uncontrollable events. The more you acknowledge that uncontrollable events happen, the more you increase your capacity to deal with them effectively.

Golden Handcuffs

As you develop a reputation for generating significant, sustainable, and profitable growth, you become a highly sought-after executive. Financial and material dreams start to come true. You move into your dream home, go on a couple of terrific family vacations a year, send your kids to the best schools, live in the best neighborhoods, and provide an extraordinary standard of living for your family. One day you realize your company is merely generating short-term earnings without feeding a sustainable business strategy. You're torn. Do you push back your boss, rock the boat, and risk your lifestyle? Do you play it safe and assume everything will work out? Do you try to influence other people to accelerate the sustainable growth of the business? Do you simply share your concerns in private whining sessions over a few drinks with your peer group? If you are a corporate catalyst, you know the answers.

Unpredictable Impact

What worked beautifully with one group to generate better results fails miserably with the next group. You give a speech one day and receive rave reviews. You give the exact same speech the next day and people won't even make eye contact with you. Just as an author, film producer, baseball pitcher, or singer cannot predict with absolute certainty how any given performance will turn out, no corporate catalyst knows for certain what strategy, method of influence, or new hire will work successfully. Like all great performers, the corporate catalyst keeps trying and makes adjustments.

No Cookie-Cutter Formulas to Follow

This one frustrates some employees so much they simply don't know what to do. They desperately want a step-by-step explanation on how to improve results. These employees repeatedly say, "Just tell me what to do, and I'll go do it." They want the room to say, "We failed because the steps were wrong." Unfortunately, they become commodities in their organizations far faster than they realize.

The corporate catalyst works to clarify the highest priority business outcomes and provides the leadership and management necessary to improve them. He or she knows there is no foolproof approach and comfortably makes adjustments.

Concentration Maintenance

Raising the performance bar in an organization excites a lot of people. It's not really that different from the local sports team winning the championship and creating excitement throughout the community. However, as the old saying goes, "Staying on top is harder than getting there." Going to work every day for years and influencing people to think in ways that drive better results can result in mental exhaustion. Burnout and boredom are real issues for corporate catalysts.

Consequently, corporate catalysts find ways to reenergize their batteries. They take several breaks within a given day or week to refresh themselves mentally for the climb ahead.

Fluctuating Popularity

When people realize a really terrific managerial leader is taking over their group, they get excited. Hope is renewed for a brighter future. If results improve steadily, their excitement grows. However, when the manager makes decisions that negatively affect these employees in the short term, their adoration wears off.

If you start to get a lot of acclaim from your group, you may get addicted to it. You may get used to people smiling at you and greeting you with open arms. Dealing with a loss of popularity can blow away your ego and cause you to reconsider your decisions and approaches. Corporate catalysts avoid these internal struggles by not attaching any value to popularity. If people like them, fine. If they are not well liked, that's okay with them as well. Ironically, the less a manager cares about popularity, the more respect he or she usually gains.

Why Bother Being A Corporate Catalyst?

People only change their behaviors when they clearly understand what is in it for them. You won't become a corporate catalyst unless you understand and buy into the rationale for being one.

6 Reasons to Be a Corporate Catalyst

1. Better income security, better career options.

First, you gain better income security, more important projects to manage, more positive attention from your employer and the competition, and more attractive career opportunities.

Approximately 300,000 IT jobs have shifted from the United States to other nations in recent years. These technical positions have become commodities in many cases. Yet, managers who convert resources into better results and effectively influence the people around them are still in demand. They may lose their job, but their ability to generate a good income is secure. In the article "The Future of Work: Flexible, Creative and Good With People? You Should Be Fine in

Tomorrow's Job Market" (*BusinessWeek*, March 22, 2004), the authors wrote:

> Changes in the economy in recent years have made some people more valuable and secure than ever.... What makes the difference? New research by economists at Massachusetts Institute of Technology and Harvard University concludes that the key factor is whether a job can be "routinized" or broken down into repeatable steps that vary little from day to day. By comparison, the jobs that will pay well in the future will be ones that are hard to reduce to a recipe. These attractive jobs require flexibility, creativity and life-long learning.

Being a corporate catalyst is very hard work, but you create a role for yourself that will be very, very hard to replace and is highly sought after.

2. Know your career has meaning.

Much more than just earning a check, you realize you make a difference. You look at each day as your canvas for painting the kind of impact you want to deliver. You know you help good things happen in your organization. If you get fired, you know you kept the behaviors you believe in and you strengthen your self-esteem for future opportunities. The day before his assassination, Dr. Martin Luther King, Jr., said his only goal was to leave a committed life behind. He was a legendary catalyst who had a very simple goal: make a difference in the world every day.

3. The intrinsic value of leadership.

If you truly care about your coworkers, you realize the greatest contribution you can make to your group is to step forward as an influencer, not backward into a realm of comfort and ease. It's hard and uncomfortable work trying to effectively influence other people, but you find out it's worth it over the long term.

4. Skill expansion.

As you accelerate your organization's highest priority outcomes, you learn new ideas and expand your understanding of individuals and groups. You increase your capacity to be effective in future groups.

5. Broaden your understanding of your career.

By taking the long-term view of your organization, you also take the long-term view of your career. You realize you don't need daily applause and immediate spectacular results to build a truly significant career. This "big picture" approach to making a difference over the long run sustains you even when it feels like you do mundane work. You don't feel the need to chase every opportunity on the horizon in order to feel good about yourself. This greatly reduces the pressure of needing daily recognition and affirmations from other people. When I was hyperventilating about grades after my first semester in high school, my freshman year counselor said, "High school is a marathon, not a sprint." He was right then, and he would be right about your career now. As a corporate catalyst, maintain the long-term perspective.

6.   Help others succeed.

Ultimately, you help other people see what they can achieve and how they can achieve it. In this manner, you not only improve your organization, you also positively impact other employees and the people they influence. You generate a legacy of high achievement not just for yourself, but for many others as well.

What reasons do *you* see for being a corporate catalyst? Make your list as long as you want. Your reasons are far more important than mine.

THE CORPORATE CATALYSTIC CONVERTER

☑   The depth and breadth of the corporate catalyst.

Essentially, a corporate catalyst is a very effective manager and leader. He or she influences other people in ways that generate more productive behaviors while simultaneously creating an environment where employees convert available resources into better results.

☑   Understanding it's work and it's worth it.

The corporate catalyst understands accelerating an organization is very hard work and is very much worth the effort.

Recommended Resources for Corporate Catalysts

The Effective Executive by Peter Drucker (HarperCollins, 1966). This is one of the classic books written by the ultimate corporate catalyst. Drucker explains how to effectively analyze your use of time, leverage your strengths, and make productive decisions. This is a must-read for anyone wanting to be a corporate catalyst.

II

The
Tools

Chapter 3

LABELS DON'T LEAD

WE'RE LIVING THROUGH a historically steep leadership learning curve. Unfortunately, we're learning from unbelievably poor examples of leadership. Senior-level executives in a wide variety of major corporations deceived members of their organizations at an extraordinary pace. There was a time when people assumed CEOs of major corporations were great leaders. The rationale was, "If this person is the CEO of a major company, then he or she must be a great leader. How else could he or she have received that position?" People no longer make that assumption.

During this intense focus on corporate leadership, a number of valuable lessons emerged. The most important lesson I learned is that labels don't lead. Having a certain title does not make a person a great leader. Leadership can come from anywhere in an organization, but it is not guaranteed to come from the top executive. The basic premise of this book is that any person in a corporation can provide the leadership necessary to accelerate critical business outcomes. Therefore, all employees need to understand the myths about leadership, what leadership really means, and how to effectively lead.

Leadership Mythology

I put the word "leadership" in an Internet search and came up with 7,567,613 entries. In trying to narrow the list, I entered "books on leadership." That generated 1,244,937 entries. Apparently there is no lack of information on leadership. However, my observations inside a wide variety of organizations convinced me that many leadership mantras are fallacies.

9 Myths About Leadership

1. People want to be led.

No, they don't. Many people say they want a great new leader, but they really want certain outcomes and would love for someone to provide a silver bullet for achieving those outcomes. However, these people don't want someone trying to guide them to do what might be uncomfortable for them. Warren Bennis wrote about this phenomenon in his book, *The Unconscious Conspiracy: Why Leaders Can't Lead* (AMACOM, 1975). Effective leaders, the corporate catalysts, understand this fallacy.

2. Leaders are born.

Nobody comes right out and says this, but a lot of times, people act like they believe it. When a person emerges from the pack as a leader, others denigrate their accomplishments by saying, "Well, of course, she's a leader. Look at her parents." Or someone will say, "I knew all along he was going to be a leader. He's got good genes." Huh? Does that mean other people just have to suck air? Leadership is a learned skill, not a hereditary gift. Unless you understand this, you may give up on becoming a leader.

3. Leaders make the final decisions.

Not always. This fallacy implies that leaders automatically have the highest title in any group. That's not true. Many times, the highest-ranking executive got there because he was great in sales, operations, or marketing. However, being a great salesperson does not automatically equate to being a great leader. The other problem with this fallacy is that it causes people to refrain from leading until their label changes. This is the corporate catch-22: a person can't get promoted unless they're a leader, but they can't lead unless they have been promoted. Doesn't make any sense, does it? When I meet a new client and the senior executives are introduced as "the leaders of this company," I always think to myself, "Prove to me you're a real leader and not just a label."

4. If you get the results, your approach doesn't matter.

Pretty amazing how good short-term results can disguise extraordinarily poor leadership, isn't it? This myth invaded far too many organizations in the late 1990s and early 2000s.

Here's an excerpt from a memo dated July 1, 2000, from Ken Lay, chairman of the board, to all employees at Enron:

> As officers and employees of Enron Corp., we are responsible for conducting the business affairs of the Company in accordance with all applicable laws and in a moral and honest manner. To make certain that we understand what is expected of us, Enron has adopted certain policies, with the approval of the Board of Directors, all of which are set forth in the enclosed booklet. Please note that Enron has provided further description of our Business Ethics policy with respect to our legal contracts. I ask that you read them carefully and completely and reflect on your past actions to make certain that you have complied with the policies. It is absolutely essential that you fully comply with these policies in the future.
> (*Source:* St. Louis Post-Dispatch, November 24, 2003)

This memo came out at exactly the same time as some Enron executives conducted incredibly corrupt behaviors. Corporate catalysts understand their behaviors and decisions are just as important as their short-term results in generating significant, sustainable, and profitable growth.

5. Leaders are motivators.

I read this one all the time, but it's not true. Motivation is an intrinsic affair. Leaders can help people realize why certain behaviors would be more beneficial, but no one can motivate someone to do something they don't want to do. By dismantling this fallacy, you take a lot of pressure off of yourself. Just know you can't motivate other people; they can only motivate themselves.

Faculty Input From "Corporate Catalysts University"

In an interview in the October 27, 2003, *USA Today*, Lorin Maazel, music director of the New York Philharmonic, said:

> In rehearsal a lot of conductors mess up by stopping to say something, but when they start again it sounds exactly as it did before. If you want to make a difference, never say anything that's not going to make a difference.
>
> Emotion is what it's all about. Music making without emotion and passion is nothing. Fine orchestras respect themselves and have a great sense of mission and esprit de corps. They're trying to do their best. Nobody's perfect. I'm never looking for a perfect performance. I'm looking for an impassioned performance. I know that no one wants to do anything but his best. If he doesn't, I don't frown and complain. Don't demand perfection. Demand passion.

Essentially, Maazel allows his performers the opportunity to regain themselves, free themselves of what is getting in the way, and allow their passion to surface again. He realizes the motivation is already within these individuals. He doesn't try to motivate people. He creates an environment where motivated people succeed.

6. Leaders are tall.

Talk about the unconscious conspiracy. According to Steven Landsburg, author of *Fair Play: What Your Child Can Teach You About Economics, Values and the Meaning of Life* (Free Press, 1997), an extra inch of height can be worth an extra $1,000 a year in wages, after controlling for education and experience. One argument is that taller people developed stronger self-esteem during their late teen years, and this carried over to their careers. Another argument says that people associate greater authority with height because of the days when humans lived with animals and size was an index of power and strength. It has been more than 100 years since a U.S. president was shorter than the average man.

Having said that, it's a ludicrous myth. Height and body size do not cause one person to be a better leader than another person. Self-esteem is a critical issue for leading effectively, but every individual can strengthen or weaken their self-esteem. The same is true with being an effective leader. If height was a factor in leading effectively, there would be no great leaders shorter than the average man or woman. That would eliminate Mother Theresa and Mohandas Gandhi as potentially great leaders. Throw out this fallacy before it impedes your ability to lead or let others lead.

7. Leaders are men.

Fast Company magazine had an article called "Where Are the Women?" (February 2004) that analyzed why so few women make it all the way to the top of large corporations. While the percentage of women executives has grown dramatically in the past 10 years, the percentage of female CEOs is astonishingly low. Also, only 15.4 percent of all corporate officers in Fortune 500 companies are women. Based on these statistics, one could assume this means women just don't have what it takes to lead large corporations.

However, the authors of the articles dug deeper, interviewed hundreds of female executives and found the vast majority of them simply do not want to live the all-encompassing 24/7 travel and work life of a CEO at a major corporation. Based on this, one could assume women are smarter in the big scheme of things than men. Does this desire to have a life outside of work make these women less capable of leading? I don't think so. I believe men and women are equally capable of being great leaders.

Case Study: The Whistle-Blowers

In the midst of extraordinary corporate and government corruption, three women were named the 2002 Persons of the Year by *Time* magazine. Were they CEOs? Nope. Did they achieve unbelievable sales results? Uh-uh. Were they the top operations person in their organization? No. What did they do to earn this prestigious award? They did the right thing. They stood up to their bosses and told them they were doing the wrong thing.

Coleen Rowley wrote to her boss at the FBI and warned that Zacarias Moussaoui, a coconspirator of the September 11th terrorist attack, must be investigated—long before the attack occurred. She then made it known to the FBI director that she was ignored. Cynthia Cooper told the board at WorldCom that the company had covered up $3.8 billion in losses through phony bookkeeping. Sherron Watkins was the Enron vice president who wrote a letter to Ken Lay, chairman of Enron, that the company's methods of accounting were improper. These three women provided extraordinary leadership by challenging their bosses. They operated behind the scenes and risked their careers to do the right thing. *That* is leadership.

8. Leadership flow follows the org chart.

Ever hear someone say that you should follow the chain of command, do not go around your boss, and don't skip levels unless you want to undermine the authority of the person below you? Makes it sound like corporations are made up of 18th century militaries where people can't communicate to one another for days.

That's not what it's like in a corporation. You work every day in cross-functional groups. You work with customers and suppliers and people who rank higher than you and those who rank lower than you. The modern organizational chart looks like Figure 3.1.

The Modern Organizational Chart

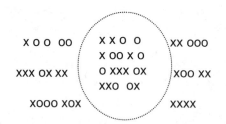

Figure 3.1

The *X*s represent people who work inside your company including your CEO, your peers, your staff members, and other department members. The *O*s represent people outside your company, including suppliers, customers, competitors, and people from other industries. The dashed line represents the facilities of your company. As you can see, employees from all departments mix together with suppliers, customers, competitors, and people from other industries. These interactions happen inside your company's facilities and out in the marketplace. At any given moment, you could be with any conglomerate of people. You can't put making a difference on hold while waiting for the official org chart to reassemble. You need to be a "360-degree leader" and influence people in every direction—your boss, your peer group, your direct reports and their staff members, your suppliers, your competitors, and even your customers.

9. **Leaders are charismatic speakers; no, wait, they're shy and introverted.**

For many years, people expected corporate leaders to be bigger than life, charismatic, dynamic, and inspiring figures who could generate better business results simply by walking into the room and sharing a few pearls of their wisdom. In some situations, tone and inflection were more important than strategy and execution. How this Hollywood image of leadership became corporate reality is beyond my comprehension, but it lasted for years and years.

Then Jim Collins's book *Good to Great* (HarperBusiness, 2001) came out. Collins went so far to prove charismatic leadership was not a prerequisite for sustainable and profitable success that he unintentionally deified the shy, introverted, and humble leaders. Unfortunately, he re-created the exact same myth that leaders have to have a specific personality. Instead of searching for the corporate version of John F. Kennedy, corporations started looking for the reincarnation of Robert Young from the TV series *Father Knows Best*. Either way, the idea that leaders need to have a certain personality is a myth. I've seen loud ones and quiet ones, friendly ones and stiff ones, and leaders who were visionary orators as well as leaders who wouldn't step behind a microphone if their lives depended on it.

The Value of Understanding Leadership Myths

What's the point of understanding these leadership myths? It's to realize that anyone can be an effective leader in a corporation.

Regardless of their title, height, gender, race, upbringing, or personality, any person in an organization can be an important leader. Personally, I find that to be liberating. Hope you do, too. It means you can be a critically important leader in your organization today.

Defining Leadership

In order to become a leader, it helps to know what leadership means. Otherwise, you can invest a lot of time and energy into activities that don't make your company more successful. Here's my definition of leadership:

Leadership means influencing how people think in ways that generate better sustainable results for your organization and the individuals in it.

Notice, leadership is an action, not a description. Dr. Martin Luther King, Jr., was a leader. He influenced people through his speeches, books, letters, and behaviors. Mohandas Gandhi was the opposite of Martin Luther King in many ways. He was frail and terribly shy. The first time he stood up to speak, he looked at the audience, became frightened, and sat back down. He influenced the way people thought through his integrity and personal sacrifices. Mother Theresa was a great leader. She didn't have a big title or receive a high income. She lived among the poorest people in the world. She influenced the way people thought through her sincerity and her actions.

We all know these three people were great leaders. However, we often overlook what made them great leaders and how it applies to all employees inside corporations. What they had in common is they each influenced how other people thought in ways that generated extraordinary outcomes. Once you understand this, you can quickly move toward being an effective business leader, regardless of your labels, because everyone can influence the way other people think. To be a great business leader, you must influence the people around you to accelerate the achievement of your organization's HPOs in a sustainable way that is effective both for the organization and the people in it.

How Successful Business Leaders Effectively Influence People

The remainder of this chapter explains a variety of ideas on leadership including:

- A breakdown of how to meet the personality needs of different people.

- A process for focusing the other person on generating better results in hs or her highest priority business outcome.

- Twenty simple ways to influence other people in any situation.

- An analysis of how to be successful in a variety of typical business leadership opportunities.

Meet Their Personality Needs, Not Yours

Leaders do not have a particular personality style. However, and this is a very big *however*, they do meet the personality needs of other people. If you fall into the "I don't have time to figure everybody else out, they'll just have to learn to do it my way" category, you missed the following key point about leadership: leaders influence the way *other* people think. If you can't meet the other person's personality needs, you'll probably never get the opportunity to influence their thought process. Keep the big picture in mind. You want better business results, not a satisfied ego.

Basically, there are four types of decision-makers: quick, emotional, logical, and conscientious. I first learned about this general topic from *Social Style/Management Style: Developing Productive Work Relationships* by Robert Bolton and Dorothy Gorver Bolton (AMACOM, 1984) and from the DISC personality assessment from Carlson Learning Center. You probably have seen similar information, but it's important to make sure this foundation on personality needs is in place. Here are three key points on the issue of meeting personality needs:

- Don't stereotype personality types to jobs. Some people assume engineers have one personality type, CEOs have

one personality, salespeople are all the same, administrative assistants are the same, and so on. It's not true.
I've done well over 150 seminars on this topic. Each time
I ask the participants to write down the one decision-
making personality type that best describes them in a
work situation. Invariably, the group has representatives
for each type. No matter how similar their titles or years
of experience, these individuals still flow into all four
categories.

♦ Don't assume an individual retains the same personality
type in all situations. A quick decision-maker may turn
conscientious if the decision at hand could determine the
career fate of a hundred employees. Consequently, you
need to stay alert all the time. You just can't assume the
same approach to meeting personality needs will work
with the same person over and over again.

♦ Again, the goal is not to get other people to meet your
personality needs. Your objective is to first meet their
personality needs, regardless of their title, so you can
move toward influencing the way they think. You can't
influence someone if they ignore you.

4 Types of Decision-Makers and How to Meet Each of Their Needs

Quick Decision-Maker

Quick decision-makers are impulsive types of people. They communicate in a very direct, strongly opinionated, decisive, and forceful
manner. They believe "my way is the right way." In general, they do
not listen very well, do not want to see a lot of paperwork, and must
immediately see the value you bring or they will decide to move on
without you. The most important thing to a quick decision-maker is
that a decision gets made immediately. Archie Bunker from *All in the
Family* was an example of a quick decision-maker.

How do you meet the needs of a quick decision-maker?

Listen more than talk. Be direct and to the point. Convince, but don't command. Expect abruptness and rudeness. Provide the person with three options and ask which one they think would be the most appropriate. Invariably, the quick decision-maker will choose one of the options and make a few changes to it. As long as these changes fit within your parameters, go along with them. Limit socializing and avoid conversation about the weather and your family unless they bring it up first. Be brief, confident, and focused. Follow up your conversation with a half-page summary in bullet point format.

Emotional Decision-Maker

Emotional decision-makers are excitable types of individuals. They like social conversations about nonbusiness issues. They really enjoy getting to know what makes you tick, where you grew up, and what you enjoy doing away from work. They very much want the relationship to feel right before moving on to business topics. They want to be excited about working with you. They despise paperwork and want communication to be conversational. The most important thing to an emotional decision-maker is for them to feel excited about the decision. Jimmy Stewart as George Bailey in the film *It's a Wonderful Life* represents emotional decision-makers.

How do you meet the needs of an emotional decision-maker?

Be casual and friendly. Start off with nonbusiness topics. If you jump to business topics too quickly, this person will feel you don't really care about them as an individual. Use their name often. Relax, smile, and stay upbeat. After you've given a reasonable amount of time to social topics, find a way to shift the conversation to business. Emphasize the importance this person brings to the project. Use handwritten note cards to follow up with them.

Logical Decision-Maker

Logical decision-makers want to move from point A to point B in seven very logical steps. They want to see how all of the pieces fit together before they make a decision. They listen more than they talk, do not like quick changes, and avoid conflict. They have controlled mannerisms, stay very formal, and analyze facts before making a decision. They want to know why you recommended your suggestions. They enjoy going through paperwork. The most important thing to a logical decision-maker is for the decision to make sense. Spock in the television series *Star Trek* is an example of a logical decision-maker.

How do you meet the needs of a logical decision-maker?

Keep your emotions in check. Explain step-by-step how, together, the two of you will move from point A to point B to point C. Use a flowchart or a giant puzzle to show how all of the different components fit together. Have your explanation typed up with copies for each of you and visually walk the person through the process. Be methodical and patient. Follow up your conversation with a clear, step-by-step and typed summary of the discussion.

Conscientious Decision-Maker

Integrity is everything to this person. People who are conscientious decision-makers want to be absolutely certain that working with you is the right thing to do. They want proof you follow the rules and do what you say you will do. They are organized, formal, and very difficult to change. They will test you openly in front of other team members as to whether you do things the right way. They like to look at information privately for a long period of time. Several days or weeks later, they will come back and present their decisions to you. The most important thing to a conscientious decision-maker is for their decision to be the right decision. Alan Greenspan represents the conscientious decision-makers.

How do you meet the needs of a conscientious decision-maker?

Keep your emotions in check. Sell your "track record" with testimonials from past customers and team members on why your approach worked successfully. Have phone numbers and e-mail addresses for references available so they can validate your information. Provide hard facts backed up by statistical reports. Expect them to want the information to be perfect. Be ready to provide them with key information. Do not wing it. If you don't know an answer, don't make one up. They will check up on you. Be very patient with them as they develop their decision. Give them plenty of time to examine the information without you being present. Be sure your follow-up is accurate and backed up with facts.

A Sample of Meeting Personality Needs

When you try to move the members of your group toward any desired outcome, step back and analyze how you will meet the needs of all four types of decision-makers. For example, if you want to sell the value of using a new purchasing procedure to a group of department heads, you could do the following:

♦ For quick decision-makers, provide opportunities for one-on-one conversations that last no more than 20 minutes. Provide them with three options of how they could implement the new program and ask which one they prefer. If the other person makes modest modifications to one of the options, go along with it.

♦ For emotional decision-makers, give them time to talk about social topics. Then discuss how exciting this new program will be for the company and how it will allow people more time to interact with each other and not be so tied to the paperwork.

♦ For logical decision-makers, provide a detailed written explanation of the steps required for execution, the timeline for executing those steps, and the rationale for using this new system.

♦ For conscientious decision-makers, explain how this system has been used in other companies and how it has decreased the number of mistakes. Have a list of references with contact information for these people to use.

Solution Leadership

Solution Leadership is an approach for improving results without telling the other person what to do. A more traditional name would be the "Socratic Approach," which is based on Socrates's ability to use questions as a means of generating better results. In essence, this is the indirect approach to improving outcomes. Rather than telling the other person what to do, you ask a series of questions and exchange ideas in a collaborative manner to generate the action plan. In many situations, you achieve your desired results far faster by using an indirect approach than a direct approach. The reason is because people don't want to be told what to do. They want to feel they played a role in developing the solution. If you tell them what to do, their subconscious wall may go up and they won't hear you.

The Eight Steps of Solution Leadership

1. Clarify the HPO.

Ask the other person, "What is the highest priority business outcome you want us to achieve this quarter?" Make sure his answer is a desired business outcome and not an internal activity. For example, if he says, "Our HPO is improved teamwork," you can ask, "If teamwork is improved, what business result do you believe we will impact? Will it be improved retention of customers, increased market share, attraction of new customers, or some other business outcome?"

2. Ask how this objective fits within the framework of your organization's business priorities.

Make certain the members of your group work on things having a direct impact on what your organization wants to achieve. If your organization's business plan says, "Increase percentage of business from current customers," a good HPO for a sales group member could be, "Increase number of products sold per customer," and a good HPO for an operations group member could be, "Expand product line to meet customer needs at different price points." Keep discussing the HPO with the other person until it fits clearly within your organization's business plan.

3. Ask clear, open-ended, and value-driven questions.

Ask a series of open-ended questions to get the other person thinking about how to generate the desired business outcome. For example, you might ask, "If you could change or improve three things about what we're currently doing that would get our current customers to buy from us more often, what would you recommend we do and why did you choose those answers?" Make sure your question focuses on improving the HPO. You may want to give the question to the other person a few days before your meeting so she can think through her answers.

4. Pause while the other person is thinking, and wait patiently while he crafts his answers.

Even if the other person has already seen the question, be patient after you ask it and let him organize his thoughts. If necessary, repeat the question, but refrain from interjecting your thoughts. By staying quiet, you give the other person the opportunity to think. If you answer the question for him, you are not leading. Remember, leadership means influencing how other people think. If you give them the answers, they don't have to think.

5. Offer your ideas on the topic.

The other person will be much more likely to listen to your ideas if you let her share her ideas first. After she has given her input, offer your ideas in the form of suggestions. Don't act as though your ideas are better than hers. This is not a competition. The goal is to generate better results, not to win an argument.

6. Discuss all of the ideas that have been shared and see if either of you can combine two or more ideas together to make an even better idea.

Keep collaborating until you both feel you have generated good, solid ideas for achieving the desired outcome.

7. Facilitate a discussion on establishing an action plan.

Ask, "Now that we've identified some ways to achieve our goal, what steps do you think we need to take over the next three weeks to make it happen?" You can adjust that time frame to your situation. Another key question to ask is, "Whom do you need to influence in order to execute this plan effectively?" Once the other person identifies key individuals, say, "Let's start with that first name. Specifically, how will you influence him (or her)?" Keep using open-ended questions and a collaborative approach to clarify what each of you will do after the meeting is over.

8. Follow up regularly.

One good conversation does not improve business results. Corporate catalysts know they have to stay engaged in the relationship in order to move the needle forward on results. The follow-up conversation can be centered on very basic questions, such as:

- What did you do since we last met?
- What worked well?
- What did not work well?
- What did you learn?
- What adjustments will you make the next time?
- What are you going to do now?

Take turns answering these questions so that each of you better understands what happened. You and your partner can exchange suggestions on what to do next. Then, together, clarify the next steps and move back into action.

Solution Leadership is an approach for influencing how other people think, which you can use regardless of your title or the title of the other person. It has nothing to do with "position power." You lead by asking open-ended questions, engaging the other person in a collaborative conversation, and working together toward improving the HPO.

Tools of Influence

Leadership is a skill and, consequently, it can be honed. This section contains 20 different ways to influence the way other people think. You will notice they are very simple ideas. That's the point. Being a great leader is not complicated. It's a matter of applying the basic tools of influence over and over again.

20 Ways to Influence People

1. Act with integrity.

Do what you said you would do, do what you believe is the right thing to do, and always be honest. If you do those three things all of the time, people will trust you. They may not always like you, but they will trust you. When you build trust, you have the capacity to influence other people. If you lie one time, they will always wonder if you're telling the truth.

2. Ask questions and listen.

Simply by asking a question, you guide the conversation in a specific direction. Effective questions immediately involve the other person in the movement toward better results. Use open-ended questions rather than yes-or-no questions. The former stimulates conversation, while the latter stifles it.

3. Provide an analogy that resonates with the other person.

By listening, you learn more about the other person. You find out about his or her hobbies, passions, and past experiences. Once you know these things, you can personalize your analogies. For example, I coached a vice president of marketing who was a track star in college. He was very proficient in his work, but often found it difficult to stay focused while other departments presented their reports. When we spoke privately after the meeting, I steered the conversation away from the work group and toward his track days. I said, "If you won your race, does that mean your team won the meet?" He said, "Of course not. I could win and the team could lose." I responded, "Right. The same is true with your business group. Your department could do well, but if the operations department, the technology department, and the human resources department are not successful, your business could go down."

He began to ask other department heads how he could help them achieve their individual objectives. Together they created a far more effective cross-functional work group and business results steadily improved. Find the other person's special interests and build your input around what appeals to him or her.

4. Make a bold statement.

This represents one of the sexier leadership tools and gets most of the media acclaim. Martin Luther King's "I have a dream" challenge and John F. Kennedy's "We will have a man on the moon by the end of the decade" declaration are famous more than 40 years later because they were bold, concise, and compelling. If it is used sparingly, this tool can be very effective. In the film *Apollo 13*, the head of operations for NASA said, "Failure is not an option." That bold statement caught the imagination of everyone in the room. You can do the same for your group.

5. Model the desired behavior.

If you want to create a certain type of corporate culture, serve as a role model. If you want people in your group to listen better, really listen to them. When someone says, "Dan, I told that person he needs to ask more questions," I repeat what I heard. I say, "You told him to ask questions. I doubt he heard you because your actions spoke louder than your words. Instead of telling him to ask questions, what would you think about asking him what he sees as the benefit of asking questions and then listening to what he says?"

6. Share a personal story.

Personal stories humanize the leadership process. They're even more useful if you poke a little fun at yourself. If you make yourself out to be a hero every time, the story loses some of its impact. Be sure your story has relevance to the other person's situation.

7. Build trust through open and honest dialogue.

Shoot straight with other people. Don't tell them what you think they want to hear. Tell them what you think they need to hear. Of course, tact and timing can go a long way in this category.

8. Demonstrate that you believe in their ability to succeed.

Give the other person the chance to fall on their face. If the scheduled speaker at a big corporate meeting calls in sick, turn to this person and give him or her the opportunity to close out the meeting rather than doing it yourself. When you demonstrate that you trust others, you create an environment for motivated people to thrive. Remember, you can't motivate anyone to do what he or she doesn't want to do, but you can create an environment where motivated people can step forward and succeed.

9. Challenge others to do even better.

More than 50 years ago, Jimmy Carter interviewed for a position in the Navy's Nuclear Submarine program with Admiral Hyman Rickover. Rickover asked about Carter's performance in school. Jimmy Carter bragged about his high ranking and outstanding performance. Then Admiral Rickover asked, "I understand you did very well, but was it your best?" Carter wanted to say it was his best effort, but he recalled times when he gave less than his all. He said, "No sir, I didn't always give it my best effort." Admiral Rickover looked him in the eye and provided the most important question in Carter's life by asking, "Why not your best?" Carter said that challenging question stimulated his thinking for the rest of his career, even beyond his term as president. It drove his performance all the way to the Nobel Peace Prize (*Why Not the Best?* by Jimmy Carter, Bantam Books, 1976).

What question or statement could you use to challenge your peers, your direct reports, or even your boss? For starters, you could ask, "Is this the best you're capable of doing?"

10. Step way out of your comfort zone.

Sam Walton wore a grass skirt and Hawaiian shirt and did the hula dance on Wall Street in 1984 because he lost a bet that "we couldn't possibly produce a pretax profit of more than 8 percent" (*Sam Walton: Made in America*, Doubleday, 1992). Walton wrote, "Most folks probably thought we just had a wacky chairman who was pulling a pretty primitive publicity stunt. What they didn't realize is that this sort of stuff goes on all the time at Wal-Mart. We always have tried to make life as interesting and as unpredictable as we can."

What out of the ordinary thing can you do to drive home your point? What would be totally out of character for you to do that would catch people's attention and influence them to think differently? Keep your integrity, but have some fun with this one.

11. Clarify with other people the risks and the rewards of taking action.

Sometimes people don't take action because they either don't understand the benefits or overestimate the risks. Before trying to get the members of your group into action, ask, "What are the benefits if we do this, and what is the biggest danger we face if we do it?" Increase your group's awareness about what is really at stake.

12. Help the group to define what they will do *and* what they will not do.

This is mission critical. Far too often I've seen executives get excited and turn their staff members on to a new project without ever identifying what activities will need to stop. Regardless of your title, you can say, "That really sounds exciting. I can't wait to get started. What three things do you think we need to stop doing so we have the time, energy, and money to do what needs to be done in this new project?" By providing this leadership, you save everyone a ton of frustration in the long run.

13. Clarify the impact your group can have on other people if they succeed.

Make a list of all the groups your team could positively affect. Get as much involvement in this process as you can. The more people realize they work on projects much bigger than just themselves, the more likely they will pour their hearts into executing them successfully.

14. Provide a book or film that causes other people to think differently.

You probably have been given dozens of free books over the years with the comment, "I think you should read this." How many of those books ever get read? If you really want to influence another person through a book, suggest a specific 10 to 15 pages for them to read. That approach has a large upside: the person might actually read those few pages, the person might end up reading the whole book once they're hooked, and the person will feel you carefully selected the section for them.

Use the same approach with films. Don't pull a group of people aside to watch an entire film. They might feel you're stealing their valuable time. Instead, show a series of short clips from a variety of famous films that make a powerful and relevant point. If your group feels overwhelmed, show the opening scene from *Indiana Jones and the Raiders of the Lost Ark* where Harrison Ford narrowly escapes getting killed by a boulder only to find himself facing a huge group of natives with spears. Then say, "And you thought we had it bad."

15. Follow up periodically.

I mentioned this before, but it deserves repeating. People make the most progress after the first follow-up session. The reason is because when you follow up, the other person knows you're really serious. Invariably, the executives I work with don't accomplish what they said they would do by the first time I follow up with them. By the third time we meet, their execution rate hovers around 95 percent.

16. Let them know about your weaknesses.

If you come across as real, people are more likely to listen. Tell stories about how you failed and learned to make adjustments. In general, people will accept your input more if it comes across as something you learned from dealing with a past failure.

17. Talk about your heroes and ask about their heroes.

If you want to learn a lot about a person's values, ask them to list their heroes. Then ask them to tell you why each person is one of their heroes. It won't take long before you know what is important to them and what motivates them. Is it family, money, security, sense of adventure, or something else? When you understand a person's underlying motives, you better understand how to influence them.

18. Ask them to recall a success story from their past.

This is a biggie. I'm convinced every person has a golden nugget in his or her past and it simply needs to be brought forward in his or her mind in order to use it. Ask the other person to describe a success story from his past—at any age level and under any set of circumstances. Ask him what he wanted to achieve, what obstacles he had to overcome, how he persevered, what it felt like when he achieved his goal, and what lessons he learned along the way. Be patient and just let him think and talk. Then ask how he could use the lessons he learned from that experience toward driving better business results today.

19. Ask what advice they would give to another person who is trying to achieve the same thing.

If the person is struggling with a particular problem, ask, "What advice would you give to someone else on how to handle this situation?"

You may need to repeat that question a few times, but usually people find it much easier to give other people advice than to solve the problems on their own. After the person has given several pieces of advice, say, "This is great advice. Now, which of these pieces are you going to put into action?" By doing this, you help the person get out of his own way and you help him get back into action. *That's* leadership.

20. Ask them about their greatest strengths and passions.

Have them make lists of their strengths in their personal and professional lives. Find out what they love to do. Then ask them how they could apply their strengths and passions at work in a way that would drive better business results. This takes time, but it will help them guide their strengths and passions toward driving the desired outcomes.

The Power of the Personal Note

Give personalized, handwritten notes to applaud great behaviors and results. Use this medium to compliment, challenge, and congratulate other people. In our world of constant e-mails and voice mails, handwritten notes are more meaningful than ever before.

Corporate Catalyst Tip #3:
Learn the Craft of Leadership

Being a leader means being a craftsman. The more you use these tools of influence, the better you get at leading other people. Here's where these tools came from: I made a list of all the leaders I admire. Some were famous, but most were people from my life—my parents, teachers, coaches, bosses, and so on. Then I asked myself what they did to influence me. From that, I came up with these tools of influence. I encourage you to do the same. Recall everyone who ever effectively influenced you, analyze how they did it, and constantly add to your leadership repertoire.

Leadership Opportunities

You don't need a historically important occasion to lead. You don't have to be at a board of directors meeting to lead. You don't have to be in front of the media to lead. All you need is an opportunity to influence how people think in a way that generates better sustainable results for your organization and the people in it. Those opportunities come along every single day.

I've invested approximately 2,500 hours on-site with a variety of clients and have observed people at all levels in corporations interact in situations ranging from private conversations to small group meetings to large conferences. I've watched executives, managers, and frontline associates deal with an array of circumstances. Here are 15 such situations and my suggestions on how to provide leadership in each of them.

15 Business Situations for Providing Influence

1. The big speech.

Giving an important presentation at a big company gathering is a great opportunity to lead. To optimize your opportunity, break the speech into five parts: the weeks before the speech, the minutes before the speech, the speech, the minutes after the speech, and the weeks after the speech. Each time frame requires focus and execution.

- A few weeks before the speech, identify the desired outcome of your presentation. Ask yourself and other people, "What results or behaviors do we want improved as a result of this speech?" Until you know the desired outcome, the speech has no relevant value for the audience. It's just a data dump. Talk with five or six audience members to gain an understanding of the issues that could keep the participants from delivering the desired outcomes. Also, ask them what they see as the strengths of the audience members, which could be leveraged to achieve the desired outcome.

- In the minutes before the speech, prepare yourself mentally. Focus on providing real value for assisting the audience members to achieve the desired outcomes.

Remind yourself that the speech is for them, not for you. The more you do that, the more you relieve your internal pressure. You will worry less about what the audience is thinking about you and focus more on helping them. Cavett Robert, founder of the National Speakers Association, said the key turning point in his career was when he went from "here I am" to "there they are."

- During your speech, keep in mind two points. The first point is the age-old aphorism for speakers, "Tell them what you are going to tell them, tell them, and then tell them what you told them." Keep your remarks clear, practical, and understandable. The second point is, "The enemy of the speaker is sameness." This classic piece of advice came from the late Bill Gove, who spoke professionally for more than 50 years. A speech needs variety. If you tell great personal stories, but that's all you do, your presentation loses its impact. Weave in a variety of personal stories, famous quotes, visual aids, analogies, quotes from people in the audience, and so on. Your message resonates far longer when you use variety in your delivery.

- In the minutes after your speech, be careful of "off the cuff" comments. I once heard a speaker talk very intensely about the importance of listening. Shortly after the presentation, he admitted he wasn't really listening to an audience member, but merely demonstrating the technique of looking into their eyes. Huh? And how about the time when the wife of the governor of Maryland said, "If I had a gun, I would shoot Britney Spears. I really would." She said that at a conference on domestic violence.

- In the weeks after the speech, make sure you bring the message back to life. Everybody is very busy and inundated with hundreds of messages every day. No matter how great your presentation, people will forget the message if you don't bring it back to life via e-mails, voice mails, handwritten note cards, and so on. You have to keep the message alive for people to remember it and take action on it.

2. Facilitating a meeting.

Meetings are, by far, the most overused and underutilized aspect of corporations. It's mind-boggling to sit in a three-hour meeting with the highest-paid employees at a particular location and watch as literally nothing gets accomplished or decided. Every meeting provides the facilitator with an opportunity to lead. Just like preparing for a speech, the facilitator has work to do before the meeting, during the meeting, and after the meeting.

- ◆ A week or so before the meeting, the effective facilitator sends a clear agenda to each of the participants. If it's a three-hour meeting, the agenda should have no more than five items for discussion. Below each agenda item, the facilitator lists any pre-work the participants need to do, such as reading certain reports or talking with members of their department about a particular issue. Also, below each agenda item, the facilitator places a key question for the participants to consider and be prepared to answer. This way, the group can move quickly into discussion when the meeting starts. Finally, at the top of the agenda, the facilitator puts the key desired outcomes for the meeting.

- ◆ Facilitating a meeting can generate extraordinary insight from the group members. As the facilitator, your role is to ask clear questions, allow room for open discussion, intervene when necessary, and deliver the desired outcomes for the meeting. For example, imagine you want to increase the retention rate of your current customers. You could pull together the members of a cross-functional team and ask, "What would be the benefit of increasing the retention rate of current customers, and what would be the downside of doing that?" After the participants discuss their answers, ask, "What two things could we change or improve that would help us retain our current customers, while avoiding the risks we just talked about?" Give everyone a chance to write down their ideas, and then gather 10 or 12 answers. Create a collaborative environment by asking, "If you could combine two or more of these ideas together into a better idea, what would it be?" Do this until the group feels satisfied with the ideas they've generated. Then have them choose their three best ideas and develop an action plan for each of them.

- ◆ However, it's not enough to have a good discussion on important topics and make meaningful decisions. You need to provide a timely recap of the group's decisions, the roles and responsibilities of the participants going forward, an expected timeline of events, and the process in which people will update one another.

3. Unethical behavior by your boss.

This doesn't happen every day, but it does happen. This is a real-life career dilemma. If you push back your boss or tell others about your concerns, you risk losing your job. If you don't, you risk losing your integrity and self-esteem. Defining moments such as these separate the corporate catalysts from those with the "employee mindset." The employee mindset says, "Tell me what to do, I'll do it, and I won't rock the boat." The corporate catalyst says, "I will do whatever it takes to generate better sustainable results for the organization and the people in it." This includes risking his job.

How do you deal with an unethical boss? If his actions were not that severe, you could confront him directly, let him know what happened, and ask what he plans to do about it. However, if you don't trust him, go to his boss and the HR representative and share with them what you know. If you lose your job, you can rebuild your career. If you lose your integrity, you're toast for the long term.

4. Dealing with a crisis.

If people's lives are at stake or customer relationships are going to be ruined, assess what needs to be done, be decisive, and move into action. Real crises don't happen as often as most people think, but when they do, act quickly.

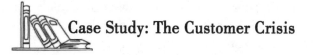

Case Study: The Customer Crisis

In a world-famous case in 1982, several containers of Johnson & Johnson's Extra Strength Tylenol were laced with cyanide, and several people died. The company immediately took all of the capsules off the shelves and replaced them. Within a few months, Johnson & Johnson exceeded their previous market share. This story has relevance more than 20 years later because it provides a great template for how to lead in a crisis: be decisive, do the right thing, and put short-term profits on the back burner.

5. Responding to poor results.

Adversity provides unlimited opportunities for leadership. When results stink and everybody points their finger at everybody else, the corporate catalyst steps in to guide the ship. Rather than focusing on the poor results, focus on analyzing how they occurred. Pull people together from different departments and ask the following questions, which is a process I call the *Bar Raising Process*:

    a. What was our original goal?

    b. What did we actually achieve?

    c. What did we do to get these results?

    d. What worked well?

    e. What did not work well?

    f. What lessons did we learn?

    g. As we move forward, what will we keep doing, what will we stop doing, and what will we start doing?

By analyzing the poor results in an objective manner, you reduce the subjective emotions flying around your group. You help people feel purposeful as they clarify what to do next.

6. Responding to great results.

Ironically, you can use this exact same approach when you encounter great results. The natural tendency is to celebrate the great results and slow down performance. However, if you use the Bar Raising Process, you convert great results into the same learning experience that poor results generated. By using this approach in good and bad times, you consistently influence other people to raise the bar and improve results in a sustainable manner.

7. Conflict between team members.

You resolve conflicts by getting those involved to move from the narrow, subjective, and emotional approach to the broad, rational, and objective mindset. Rather than having both individuals fight solely for their side of an issue, have each of them defend the first perspective and then have each of them argue for the opposite perspective.

For example, imagine the conflict is about whether a marketing executive or an operations executive should be in charge of a new initiative for improving transactions. Rather than having the two individuals provide their opposing points of view, have them work together to build a case for why a marketing person should be in charge and then why an operations person should be in charge. After they see the issue from both perspectives, ask them to work together to put a recommendation in place and explain why they believe this recommendation will add greater value to the customer.

8. Refocusing on the customer.

Far too often, companies develop and market a new product or service because someone inside the company thought it would be a good idea. Here are four points of wisdom on that topic: "You ain't the customer!"

The only way to determine the needs of customers is to step into their world, understand their objectives, and identify the obstacles keeping them from succeeding. The next time your group starts developing "good ideas that everybody will want to buy," I encourage you to intervene with this question: "What customer need or desire will this product/service meet?" Follow that question with, "How much value will a customer place on having that need or desire met?" And then bring down the hammer with, "How do you know you're right?" Keep provoking until they actually look at how customers perceive these new products and services. They can only really know by asking customers.

9. A boss who wants to keep adding more activities.

I think this is an addiction in most corporations. It's part of the Superman/Superwoman Syndrome that says, "We can do more than our competition. We have better people than they do. We can take on more and more, and still be effective." Here are three points of wisdom on that one: "No, you can't." Adding more activities to an already full plate is counterproductive.

Influencing your boss is one of the most important leadership opportunities in any organization. The next time your boss tries to load on more tactics without taking anything off your plate, say, "I see the value of this new project, and I'm honored to be part of it. Here are the six things I'm working on right now. Which ones do you want me to take off so I can focus on this new project?" Many times your boss will say, "I don't want you to stop doing any of those. I just want you to add this new one for the next 45 days or so." This brings you to the crucial moment. Keep your composure, stay very calm, and say, "The easy thing for me to do right now is to just say I'll do it. But that would be wrong for the business. It would be unfair to our customers for me to say I can do all seven of these things well simultaneously. For me to deliver the value you want delivered, we need to identify what activities are not as important. Then I can spend less time on those activities and more time on what you want."

This potentially creates a very uncomfortable conversation, but if you drop the leadership ball in this situation, you hurt your organization's results, your career, and possibly your personal life. Don't allow the desire to please your boss overwhelm your capacity to lead effectively.

10. The corporate dictate.

When a new corporate policy gets handed down to a local office, complaints such as, "What were they thinking?!" "This new compensation policy doesn't make any sense," and "The corporate big shots don't have a clue," start flying around. Obviously, the corporate dictates can throw any group off on a tangent.

These internal disruptions provide you with an opportunity to lead. The underlying issue in these situations is that employees usually feel no one listens to them or respects them. What can you do to change that feeling? I suggest you meet with the employees in small groups and say, "I just want to put together a report that summarizes our feelings and concerns, and communicates to the executives in home office what we think." Gather input from anyone who wants to offer it.

Then put together a summary of these concerns, write a cover letter, and send it to the key executives in charge of the new initiative. You can serve as the liaison between home office and your office. By doing this, you immediately provide the members of your work group with an opportunity to be heard. Even if nothing changes, they can get back to focusing on the customers.

11. Constantly shifting strategies.

Many times, executives decide employees need to do something different in order to hit the numbers required for the next quarter. This is part of the fallout from the fallacy of earnings per share. Even though a strategy concentrates on building long-term customer relationships, executives may decide to dramatically raise the price of a popular service in order to generate short-term cash flow.

What can you do to influence your boss in this situation? Don't attack his idea directly. Use an indirect approach. Say, "We can definitely make that change happen very quickly, but how does raising our prices help build long-term customer relationships? I think we need to maintain our strategic focus." Be patient and let your boss think. He or she may not do anything at the moment, but over the course of a few days, may reconsider your input. Keep bringing your boss back to the preestablished strategy. This way the discussion remains objective and rational rather than personal and emotional.

12. Being a meeting participant.

Consider the number of hours you spend in meetings every week, and you get a good idea of the number of leadership opportunities you have in front of you. When you sit in a meeting, you can interject a provocative question or statement at any moment that can influence the way people think and guide the conversation in a variety of directions. Don't overuse or abuse these opportunities. If you speak 20 times at every meeting, no one will listen to anything you say. Giving your unsolicited input two or three times in a three-hour meeting is pretty much the limit. At that rate, people know you care about the team's success and that you're willing to wade in as a leader.

When you do contribute an idea or a question, say it in a clear, concise, and compelling manner. Get in and get out quickly. The longer you ramble, the less impact you have. If it helps, write down your suggestion or question on a piece of paper and rehearse it in your mind a few times before saying it out loud. Never make a personal comment about another individual. That's enormously distracting to the group and creates an internal focus that wastes time and energy. Be willing to contribute both criticisms and compliments about ideas and execution.

13. Maintaining cross-departmental focus on an HPO.

The HPOs help guide your group's activities. If you find the participants on a project going off on multiple tangents, rein them back in with a few well-placed questions, such as, "What are the two highest priority business outcomes we are trying to achieve?" "What is the benefit of achieving these outcomes?" and "What do you need from the other departments in order to achieve the desired outcomes?" By continually pointing to the desired outcomes as the focal point, you cut off meaningless conversations that take the group on tangents.

14. Responding to a competitor's major initiative.

If your competitor suddenly gets a lot more attention from your customers, step back and evaluate what it did. If its results come from activities that do not fit within the purpose of your business, encourage the people in your organization to stick to their strategy. Chasing after a fad won't generate SSPG. Keep your team focused on executing within the definition of your business. Help team members see how investing time and energy on an idea that has nothing to do with the purpose of the business will actually hurt them more over the long term than it will help.

15. Keeping team members focused during boss transitions.

Bosses get fired or promoted constantly. If your business group loses focus every time this happens, you won't generate sustainable success. As a member of the team, help everyone stay focused while the transition takes place. Meet with colleagues informally for lunch or dinner and ask them what key outcomes they want to generate. Ask what you can do to support them and the team. Keep the conversation focused on business outcomes and supporting one another, and away from concerns about lack of stability and security.

For a short period of time, work groups can function as independent teams without a boss. The key is for someone inside of the group to step up and guide the thinking toward the customers and away from internal battles.

Each day provides real leadership opportunities. The key is for you to clarify the desired outcome, identify whom you need to influence in order to improve it, put together a plan on how you will influence each of these individuals, and move into action.

THE CORPORATE CATALYSTIC CONVERTER

☑ Understand the myths of leadership.

An extraordinary amount of literature promotes the idea that certain people are leaders and others are not. That stuff is filled with fallacies. One of the primary points of this book is that every person has the capacity to lead. The reason is because leadership is an action, not a label. Leadership means influencing how other people think in ways that generate better sustainable results for your organization and the people in it. Anyone can master the ability to influence other people.

☑ The importance of meeting personality needs.

The first step toward influencing how other people think is to meet their personality needs. If you skip this step and go directly to your desired outcome, you will fail more often than not.

☑ Leadership is an art.

There is no formula for how to lead in a given situation. Just as an artist uses different colors and brushes to create a body of work, a leader uses different approaches to influence people in different situations.

☑ Leadership opportunities are always present.

Every day you have multiple opportunities to lead. Increase your awareness of those opportunities and how you can provide influence within them.

Recommended Resources for Corporate Catalysts

The Autobiography of Martin Luther King, Jr. (Edited by Clayborne Carson, Warner Books, 1998).

This is the finest book on leadership I've ever read. I recommend it to anyone who wants to be a great leader inside a corporation. Dr. King was much more than just a great orator, he had a terrific intellect and an array of well-polished skills for influencing people.

Gandhi, An Autobiography: The Story of My Experiments With Truth by Mohandas Gandhi (Beacon Press, originally published in 1927).

This is my second favorite book on leadership. I encourage you to read it. It demonstrates clearly how a shy and seemingly frail person can influence the way people think. It is a vivid portrait of the power of modeling a desired behavior and how it can cause an entirely new culture to emerge.

Organizing Genius by Warren Bennis and Patricia Ann Biederman (Perseus Books Group,1997).

This is a unique book about the relationship between the leader and the group members in teams that existed for only two to five years. I particularly recommend pages 1–31 and 196–218. In these sections, Bennis and Biederman highlight the key findings of their research. I believe there is a great deal of relevance here for modern work groups, which oftentimes don't even last two years.

The Measure of a Man by Sidney Poitier (HarperSanFrancisco, 2000).

This is a good (but not great) book by one of my all-time favorite actors. The book actually has nothing to do with being a man or a woman. It is about leadership. Poitier rambles quite a bit, but also provides a few extraordinary stories on the power of personal integrity and how it affects our careers and the desired outcomes of our organizations.

Chapter 4

"Coach, Stay on the Sideline!"

At almost every intense basketball game, the referee turns around and yells, "Coach, stay on the sideline!" Players perform on the court, not the coaches. Wouldn't it be nice if referees existed in corporations and told managers to back off and let their employees perform? Managers fail when they tell their employees exactly what to do, or they do it themselves. These managers hurt their careers and the organization's long-term results by not trusting their employees. Micromanagers lose their best employees because these people don't want to be treated like robots or children.

The Four Responsibilities of Management

Using an Internet search engine, I found 42,466,160 entries for "management," and 4,722,877 entries for "books on management." Once again, there is no shortage of information and opinions on the other major topic in this book. One of my favorite quotes is from Oliver Wendell Holmes, who said, "I don't give a fig for the simplicity on this side of complexity; I would give my right arm for the simplicity on the far side of complexity." I believe that on the far side of management complexity, every manager has four responsibilities.

First, managers need to clarify what is expected of their employees in terms of values, strategy, short-term results, and long-term results. This is The Playing Field where their employees perform.

Second, managers need to interact with their employees on a consistent basis by asking questions, listening, offering suggestions, and pointing out things they have observed the employee doing. In this way, they provide ongoing guidance regarding the desired behaviors, strategic alignment, and results. This is all done in the spirit of assisting the employee to achieve greater success. I call this activity "coaching." Coaching, at least the way I'm defining it, does not include telling people what to do. It means working to be of value to the other person while simultaneously letting them make their own decisions.

Third, managers need to hold employees accountable for their behaviors, strategic alignment, and results. Holding people accountable includes providing both positive consequences when they operate on The Playing Field and negative consequences when they operate off it.

Fourth, the manager must stay off The Playing Field. It is absolutely counterproductive to step into the employee's area of responsibility and tell her how to behave. Even if the employee does exactly as instructed, the best the manager can hope to achieve is a short-term positive result. The employee is no better prepared for the next situation and is probably very frustrated with the manager's controlling mannerisms.

This chapter explains each of these responsibilities in detail.

A Manager's First Responsibility: Define The Playing Field

The more clearly you define the parameters for your employees, the more freedom they experience. It seems strange to generate freedom by reinforcing boundaries, but when your employees understand what is expected of them in terms of values, strategic alignment, and results, they have a great deal of freedom to make decisions and take action. When they don't know what is expected of them, they have to constantly check with you to make sure they're on the right track. The Playing Field in Figure 4.1 represents the four areas of accountability for your employees.

The Playing Field

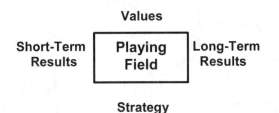

Figure 4.1

Case Study: A Contrast in Styles
From the World of Sports

Vince Lombardi and Phil Jackson served as two of the most successful coaches in the history of professional sports. Lombardi won five NFL championships with the Green Bay Packers and Jackson won nine NBA titles with the Los Angeles Lakers and Chicago Bulls. Other than that, they don't seem to have much in common. Lombardi screamed and swore at his players. He intimidated them in every way he could. Jackson focused on Zen principles and suggested books for players to read.

However, they both allowed their players to make their own decisions within a given framework. Vince Lombardi created a relatively simple running play that became known as The Packer Power Sweep. As he explained it, there were a few basic guidelines the players had to follow. Other than that, they could make decisions based on how each play unfolded. This play provided dozens and dozens of options. Similarly, Phil Jackson taught the Triangle Offense to his players. This is another simple approach to offense that provides players with a few fundamental guidelines and depends on them to make decisions as each play unfolds. He used the same basic framework, regardless of who was on the court, including Michael Jordan and Shaquille O'Neal.

These case studies provide a model for managers in terms of clarifying The Playing Field and letting employees make decisions for themselves. Here is a more in-depth description of each parameter of The Playing Field.

The Playing Field, Parameter #1: Values

Values are beliefs that determine behaviors. If you value honesty, you tell the truth. If you believe time with your family is important, you don't work 80 hours a week. This is pretty straightforward, and I'm sure you're aware of it. Here's the problem: "Corporate Values" is by far and away the management topic that gets the most lip service.

Everywhere you go you see businesses stating their Corporate Values. They're on display at restaurants, hanging over your head at the post office, and chiseled on concrete walls. Here's the dilemma: if values are beliefs that determine behaviors, behaviors inside organizations ought to reflect their Corporate Values. This is where a great deal of corporate credibility gets lost with both employees and customers. You can't preach honesty in the morning and brag about cutting corners with suppliers in the afternoon.

Here are three steps to bring Corporate Values to life in a sustainable way:

1. Gain input on the values.

When a manager comes up with a list of values and tells their employees to accept them as the group's core values, he or she automatically fails. Employees think, "Those aren't *my* values. Those aren't the things *I* believe in." Many times, employees go along with the ruse and say, "Looks good to me." Then no one, including the manager, ever brings these Core Values back up again for discussion.

In order to make the values for your work group mean something, pull together a representative set of people from your entire work group and ask, "What values are important to you in the work place?" After everyone has written down their list, put them into small teams. Have each person read off their list of values to their small group. Then have the members of each small team discuss what they heard and narrow their list to the values they think are critical for everyone in the work group to follow. This takes time and probably will require two sessions spaced apart by a few weeks. During the first session, everyone in the small group hears what the others think and there is some discussion. During the second session, everyone in the small group comes prepared to have a more in-depth discussion and decide which values should guide the behavior of the group.

2. Narrow the list to the crucial few.

Have each small team share the values they selected with all of the other small teams. The manager, or a designated person, then steps up and facilitates a discussion for narrowing all of the input from the small teams into a single set of values. Again, this requires time and patience. It may take two sessions. One, where everyone hears different points of view about each of the values, and, two, where everyone comes together to have a final discussion about the values for the entire work group.

At this point, the manager needs to bring this discussion to closure. One way to do that is to use a "5-3-1" voting approach. If you have a list of recommended values narrowed down to 12 items, have each participant vote for their three favorite values by placing a 5 next to their top choice, a 3 next to their second choice, and a 1 next to their third choice. The manager then adds up the points to determine which values matter the most to this representative group.

The manager sends this set of recommended values to all of his or her employees to gain further input. This could be done via e-mail. The message could say, "Attached are the recommended values for our work group from the committee that has been working on it. Please read over these values and provide me with your input. Which ones do you agree with, which ones do you not agree with, and what values do you think we need to add?"

The manager takes the input from all of the employees, works with the representatives to make a final decision on the values for the group, and communicates those Core Values to the entire work team. The fewer Core Values there are for the group, the better the chances of them having a positive impact on the group's behaviors.

3. Bring the values to life over and over again.

In order for these Core Values to effectively guide behaviors, the manager needs to bring them to life over and over again. Imagine that "collaboration" is one of your group's values. When you see two employees challenging each other's thought processes and developing better ideas, you can leverage this observed behavior into a more frequent happening in your organization by doing the following:

- Write each of them a note applauding their spirit of collaboration.
- At the next group meeting, highlight their behavior and ask each of them to talk about what the process was like for them.
- Mention this example in a speech to a large audience.
- Mention this example in a future newsletter.
- Give each of them a "Spirit of Collaboration" award at a group function.
- Mention this observed behavior in their annual performance reviews.

When you see examples of the desired values, do everything you can to promote them. Other people in your work group will get the message and may start behaving in the desired manner.

Quickly address behaviors that are contrary to the desired values. For example, if a person refuses to share ideas, operates in a silo separate from all other departments, and puts down other people every time they offer a new idea, step in and provide immediate consequences. Here are some suggestions:

- Meet with the person in private and let her know your concerns. Ask her why she is not more willing to share her ideas or listen to other people. Ask her what would happen if no one shared ideas. Explain how no one person can meet all of the customer's needs. Offer her some insights into the benefit of collaboration.
- In a public setting, let everyone know that keeping information and ideas in a silo is not acceptable in this culture.
- Eventually, you may need to put a note in the employee's file explaining that she is difficult to work with and not an effective team player.

♦ In a small group setting, ask each person to say what he or she needs from the others in the group in order to accelerate the achievement of the desired goal. Have this individual see that operating in a silo is not going to work in this environment.

If your group's values stay on the wall and never come to life, no one will take them seriously. A huge part of the manager's job is to make sure the group's values are taken seriously.

Corporate Catalyst Tip #4:
Values Are the Engine in Your Organization

Take your mission and values off the walls where customers can see them. These are for your employees to know, not your customers. An organization's culture is made up of the consistently displayed behaviors in the organization. If people consistently say "please" and "thank you," and really listen to one another, they have a polite, respectful culture. If they scream and swear at each other, it's not a polite or respectful culture. The values you have written on the wall do not define the culture. It is the actual, consistent, day-to-day behaviors in the organization that demonstrate the culture. Values are like the engine under the hood of your car. If the engine is working properly, the car moves. You don't drive around with your hood up so everyone can see your engine. I suggest you do the same with your organization. Keep the values under the hood and away from the customers, and let the behavior of your employees demonstrate those values.

The Playing Field, Parameter #2: Strategy

A strategy defines an organization, or a part of an organization, and the direction in which it is going. A strategy is not something you do. A strategy is a guideline for helping you to decide what to do, and, just as importantly, to decide what *not* to do. When your employees understand the strategic direction for your group, they have an important screen for their decision-making process. Before moving into action, they can ask themselves, "Does this activity fit within the strategic direction of our group?" If it does not, they shouldn't do it. This is true even if the activity would deliver the desired short-term outcome.

Of course, if they don't understand the strategic direction of your group, they will do all kinds of things to generate the desired outcomes, and, unintentionally, their efforts will take your organization all over the board. This is exactly what happens repeatedly at many organizations. A group of executives comes together and someone says, "I'm a little disappointed with these results. What can we do to make them better?" So the group brainstorms 20 ideas, narrows the list to five, converts them into an action plan, and away they go. The organization is now off and running toward improving the desired results. However, there's no strategic approach, no synergy between these activities, and no improvement in sustainable results. Employees simply work harder and longer. A year later, the executives come together and repeat the process until they are replaced by another set of executives. Rather than following this "activity-addicted" approach to business, I encourage you to use a strategic approach for deciding what to do and what not to do.

Process for establishing a strategy

1. Define desired outcome areas.

What general outcome are you trying to improve? I'm not asking for your specific numerical desired outcome. I just want to know, in general, what you want improved. Is it revenue, operating income, number of customers, retention rate of customers, revenue per customer, revenue per business unit, revenue per type of customer, or something else?

2.   Increase awareness of your business environment.

With the desired outcome area for improvement in mind, analyze your business environment. Increase awareness of your current customers and prospects. Who's buying? How much are they buying?

What are they buying? Why are they buying it? What are they not buying, and why are they not buying it? What needs do your customers have that you could address? Who is not buying from you who should be, and why aren't they?

Increase awareness of your competition. What's working for them and what's not working for them? Which customers are they getting that you want and how are they getting them? In what ways are they adding more value to customers than you?

What changes or new trends are happening in the marketplace, and how do they affect your business? What unique opportunities have been generated that you could leverage for sustainable growth?

3. Develop several potential strategies.

Begin to develop a variety of potential strategies. These are merely potential guidelines defining your part of the business and the direction it could head in. Nothing is set in stone. Do this in collaboration with other people. You'll get better ideas and better buy-in to the end product. Remember, these are not tactics for you to do, but guidelines for making decisions.

4. Select your best strategy and communicate it to the group.

Take each of your potential strategies and project it into the future. Look at how activities supporting this strategy would impact your desired outcome area for improvement. Look at how these activities would impact your overall business. Make a list of all the reasons supporting this strategy, and a list of all the reasons why your organization should not use this strategy. Go through each of your strategies and do this same analysis. Then, and this is the toughest part, select the strategy the organization, or your part of the organization, will use to guide the decisions.

Clearly explain to your employees this strategy and the rationale behind why it is being used. Explain how the group can generate far greater sustainable improvement in results when everyone operates within the same strategy. Explain there is no way to evaluate the effectiveness of a strategy unless everyone operates within it.

Strategic alignment process

Here's a three-step process for your employees to make their activities more strategic:

1. Screen every decision for strategic alignment.
   For every potential activity, decision, and meeting agenda item, they ask, "Will this support our strategy?" If they can't reasonably answer yes, they don't do it.

2. Regularly review activities for strategic alignment.
   At the end of the week, they ask themselves, "Did that activity, decision, or discussion fit with our strategy?" If it didn't, they avoid it in the future.

3. Increase strategic activities, decrease nonstrategic activities.
   As they go forward, they focus on steadily increasing the percentage of their strategic activities and decreasing their percentage of nonstrategic activities. In time, they will do less and achieve more.

Every Effective Business Strategy Is a Branding Strategy

That's a bold statement, so I put it in bold. Building a brand is about much more than advertising. It is the ultimate business strategy because it ultimately affects all aspects of a business. The more you understand the components of branding, the more effectively you will develop a strategy for your business or your part of the business.

Faculty Input From "Corporate Catalysts University"

You can't have a chapter on management without at least one quote from Peter Drucker. He wrote the following more than 50 years ago, and it is just as true today.

If we want to know what a business is, we have to start with its purpose. And its purpose must lie outside of the business itself. In fact, it must lie in society since a business enterprise is an organ of society. There is only one valid definition of business purpose: to create a customer.

Because it is its purpose to create a customer, any business enterprise has two—and only these two—basic functions: marketing and innovation.
(Source: *The Practice Of Management*, HarperPerennial, 1954)

If you put "creating a customer" and "marketing" together, you're talking about "building a brand."

We need a definition of a "brand" in order to discuss it. Here's my definition: *A brand is the perception of value a customer thinks they receive from an organization or a prospect thinks they would receive if they bought from that organization.*

In other words, your business brand resides outside of you. It resides in the minds of your customers and your prospects. Your objective is to build the perception for which you want to be known.

10 keys to remember about branding

1. A great brand is the gift that keeps on giving.

When an organization has a great brand, it means customers have a very high perception of the value they receive from it. Even when the organization occasionally misses the mark, customers give it the benefit of the doubt.

In the March 25, 2004, issue of the *Wall Street Journal*, in the article, "Investors Cut Starbucks Some Rare Slack," Steven Gray wrote, "When a top executive warns that his company won't be able to sustain its rate of growth, the result is usually a stock sell off. But that didn't happen on February 25th when Howard Schultz, Chairman of Starbucks Corp., announced that the company couldn't keep getting larger at rates as fast as 32%. Sure, the stock slipped, but only 3.4%, and then it bounced back in a day or two." Gray went on to explain that investors have such a strong perception of value regarding Starbucks because of their "long record of surprisingly good performances."

2. You build a brand from the outside-in.

You are not your customer. You don't determine for your customers whether they think you add value. Your job is to understand their needs and do the best you can to deliver value to them. However, it's their perception of the value you bring that matters, not yours. In an interesting seminar by consultant Lon Zimmerman, I learned the concept that "the customer ain't me." He compared the survey answers on a variety of topics from an advertising agency whose employees had an average age of 26 years to the answers from the general public. There were wide disparities in opinions on issues such as sex on television and favorite types of music. Zimmerman pointed out that the advertising agency has to keep in mind what is of value to its employees may not be for its target audience.

Avoid the common error of sitting in a conference room and making decisions that affect customers without having the customer perspective represented. Go out and talk with your customers frequently. The goal is not for them to figure out how to use your products or services, but for you to enhance their desired outcomes.

3.   It takes two years to build a brand.

This is one of the more interesting pieces of information I've come across in working with some of the world's best-known brands. It takes two years before customers consistently call for a new product or service by name. This is why it's so important to understand the fallacy of earnings per share. Your best brand-name product takes time to develop a reputation in the marketplace. If you throw it away and start over after six months, you just lost one of your long-term assets.

4.   It's critical to deliver more value *and* market that you deliver more value.

If you set up a new "frequent user" program that benefits your best customers, you have to let them know about it. Branding is more than just marketing, but it does include marketing.

5.   Branding is the art of sacrifice.

In order to be known for delivering a specific value, you can't be all things to all people. This is the hardest part about branding. You need to let go of a lot of things in order to be known for a few things. This takes courage to accomplish. Jim Collins wrote about this in his book *Good to Great* (HarperCollins, 2001) under the heading of "The Hedgehog Concept." He encouraged people to answer these three questions:

- What can you be the best in the world at?
- What are you passionate about?
- What drives your economic engine?

By answering these three questions, you start to narrow your focus a great deal. If you want to build a brand around your answers, you have to courageously let go of a lot of other stuff.

Faculty Input From "Corporate Catalysts University"

Helmut Panke, CEO of BMW, was interviewed in 2003 by the *Wall Street Journal*'s Neal Boudette on the topic of branding. Here's an excerpt:

> **WSJ:** BMW is one of the top brands in any industry. For you, as CEO, are there special responsibilities you have in maintaining or building your brand image?
>
> **Mr. Panke:** As provocative as it sounds, the biggest task is to be able to say, "No." Because in the end, authentic brand management boils down to understanding that a brand is a promise that has to be fulfilled everywhere, at any time. So when something doesn't fit, you must make sure that that is not done. The most important role of senior management, not just the CEO, is to understand that the brand is not just a label that you can put on and take off. BMW settles for fewer compromises, which goes back to what the brand stands for.

6. Branding does not equal a tag line.

Companies spend a lot of time and money crafting the perfect tag line. GE spent somewhere in the neighborhood of $100 million developing their tag line "Imagination at Work." Taglines are important, but they do not constitute a brand. A brand is built through operations, research, hiring certain types of people, firing certain types of people, marketing, sales, and so on. Your company's brand is the net result of the collective effort of your organization.

7. Branding is the strategy that integrates every part of your organization.

Every department in every organization should answer this question at every meeting: If we go ahead with that activity, will it support our brand? If your operations department is focused on speed, and marketing is focused on low prices, you create confusion for the customer. That's how to destroy brand equity.

8.   Give away value in order to gain opportunities.

Krispy Kreme has no national advertising budget. When they move into a new market, they give away free doughnuts to the local radio and TV stations. This helps spread the word about these tasty doughnuts. Years ago, Southwest Airlines created their Rapid Rewards program, where they gave away free flights to people who flew with them often. My favorite example is Gillette's Mach 3 razor. When they first came out with that razor many years ago, I received a free one in the mail. I still have this free razor, but I've spent a small fortune on razor blades in the meantime. What could your group give away that would strengthen your brand?

9.   Avoid ubiquity.

In the January 8, 2004, issue of the *Wall Street Journal*, Sony Corp. president Kunitake Ando was described as looking for a word in 2001 that would define his company's future direction. He dismissed "network" and "mobile," and finally settled on "ubiquity," which translated as "God is everywhere." His concept was to make Sony integrated into every aspect of the consumer's life.

He was not alone.

Keiji Tachikaway, president of NTT DoCoMo, said, "Let's put wireless devices on everything that moves." WSJ wrote, "Hitachi and other Japanese companies are making super-small chips that use radio-frequency identification technology and can be embedded in anything from dollar bills to grandmother to track the location and identity of an object or person." They've even considered putting chips in cartons of milk to tell the refrigerator when the expiration date has passed.

Here's the problem: Sony had a terrible year in 2003 with the so-called "Sony Shock," where it announced a big earnings shortfall and sliding sales in its mainstay electronics division. "Some analysts said that Sony's problems were of their own making," said Allen Wan,

Asian Bureau Chief of CBS *MarketWatch* on May 29, 2003. He reported that problems included a dearth of exciting new products and a lack of focus, as the company had interests ranging from music and movies to chips.

In the *Fortune* January 26, 2004, issue, Brent Schlender wrote, "Bill Gates, who is now ensconced as chairman and chief software architect, is determined to make Microsoft even more ubiquitous, linking all kinds of computing and communications and consumer electronic devices in a mesh of software that will make the entire Internet and everything on it a single, programmable entity." He went on to say that from January 2000 to January 2004, Microsoft's market value had fallen from $600 billion to $304 billion.

Ubiquity essentially means being all things to all people all the time. There's another word for that: commodity. It requires discipline and hard work to say no to people. It takes a lot of self-esteem to admit your group is not capable of being all things to all people. Trying to be ubiquitous involves carrying a lot of baggage, which slows down your group even more. Be clear about what value you add and what you do. Then work hard to not let other things pull you down.

10. Put "strengthen the brand" at the top of every meeting agenda.

Because branding is the ultimate business strategy, it should be the first item discussed at every meeting in every organization. The questions could go like this, "What have we done to try to strengthen our brand? What went well, what did not go well and what did we learn? What changes do we need to make to do a better job at strengthening our brand?"

The brand-building process

There's one very important question still on the table: how do you build a brand? Here's a six-step method that can be used by any organization or group.

1. Define your desired customer.

Who are you trying to serve? Until you identify your desired customer, you won't know what is of value to them. If you focus on creating something you think would be of value to you, you're doomed from the beginning. You have to know your desired customers. Write down a description of your desired customers and work to understand what is important to them.

2.   Clarify their desired outcomes.

As you research, interview, and work to understand these types of people and their perspectives, make a list of the outcomes they want to achieve. Put all of the products and services you have to offer on the back burner and focus only on what outcomes these people want to achieve. A self-cleaning oven is a product. More free time is an outcome. Financial planning is a service. Greater peace of mind is an outcome. Make a list of the outcomes your desired customers want to achieve.

3.   Identify the three highest priority customer outcomes your group can improve.

Examine the entire list of desired outcomes for these people, and identify which outcomes your group could improve. Then narrow the list to the top three customer outcomes your group will focus on improving. This is the sacrifice part I talked about earlier.

4.   Gear every decision toward delivering those three outcomes.

Make sure every member of your work group focuses on improving one or more of these three customer outcomes. This is one way to create synergistic, cross-functional teamwork that drives better sustainable results.

5.   Be boringly consistent and thoroughly innovative.

This is how you build your brand over the long term. Stay focused on improving a few customer outcomes, which can become boring. Members of your group may want to go after something new and sexy in the marketplace, but keep in mind that the greatest brands in the world stay consistently focused on a few key customer outcomes.

Just because you're focused on improving only a few outcomes doesn't mean you can't constantly get better. It just means your innovations need to improve these few desired outcomes for your customers. This dual responsibility of consistent focus and constant innovation is so important that the entire next chapter is devoted to it.

6. Market to resonate.

The final step in building a brand is to convey your brand message to your customers and prospects. If a law firm wants to be known for supporting men going through a divorce, using a famous man who went through a divorce as its spokesperson can be an effective branding approach. If that same law firm tries to represent women who are being taken advantage of by their bosses, it's a poor branding approach. Your marketing has to resonate with prospects so they clearly understand the value they would receive from your organization.

 **Case Study: The Grocery Store Example**

Here's a theoretical example on how to establish a business strategy and build a brand. Tom and Mary Smith have just become owners of a small neighborhood grocery store. They decide their number-one business goal is to increase revenues without increasing inventory. After examining their marketplace, they find the neighborhood is very ethnically diverse, has lots of families with small children, and has both a Wal-Mart and a very large grocery store nearby. They know they can't compete on price or volume or variety with the local Wal-Mart or the large grocery store. After reviewing the demographics in their area, they identify three potential strategies:

- Strategy #1: Meet the needs of the various ethnic groups.
- Strategy #2: Meet the needs of stay-at-home parents.
- Strategy #3: Meet the needs of families in which both parents work outside of the home.

After studying what needs to happen to successfully serve these different target groups, they decide to focus on Strategy #2. They study their target audience of stay-at-home parents and realize the percentage of female college graduates has exceeded more than 50 percent since the mid-1980s. They also find 13 percent more moms stay at home versus 10 years earlier. They realize American society has the most well-educated stay-at-home moms in history. They learn more dads stay at home with their children than ever before. In interviewing parents, Tom and Mary discover the prospects' desired outcomes include having peace of mind while shopping, finding ways to intellectually stimulate their children, and being able to get grocery items without leaving a sick child.

With those three outcomes in mind, the Smiths get busy. They hire a variety of stay-at-home parents to work in The Children's Center, which they built in the back of their store. They stock The Children's Center with a variety of toys and games to intellectually stimulate children at different age levels. In this manner, parents can shop peacefully while their children play. They hire local teenagers to work after school and deliver groceries to families around the neighborhood. They also emphasize hiring friendly clerks to create a family atmosphere. They reduce the number of items in their stores to basic grocery items and merchandise for family events, such as birthday parties, vacations, and picnics. They sell only books and magazines geared toward parenting issues. They label the aisles with different themes such as Breakfast, Lunch, Dinner, After School, Weekend Activities, Tools for Parents, and Birthday Parties. They put out a newsletter each month listing dates for special events at The Children's Center. They market their store as "The Parents Concierge Grocery Store."

In this manner, the Smiths leverage the resources in their neighborhood, reduce their overhead by selling fewer items, and compete with Wal-Mart by positioning themselves in a completely different manner.

The Playing Field, Parameter #3:
Short-Term Results

You should consistently evaluate your direct reports both in terms of their behaviors and their results. The first two parameters, Values and Strategy, refer to the individual's behavior. Is he or she acting in accordance with the desired values, and does his or her decisions fit strategically?

Now the focus is on results. Desired short-term results are what the individual is expected to deliver over the next month, three months, six months, and year. Meet monthly with each of your direct reports to review their performance. In addition to discussing what has already been achieved, clarify with them their expected short-term results going forward. It's important there is no confusion about these desired results.

In order to increase buy-in from your direct reports regarding these results, make this a collaborative process. Ask them what results they think they can deliver over the next 30 days, 90 days, and 180 days. Make sure these objectives connect to the overall desired results for your organization so the individual doesn't go on a tangent. If her objectives align with the organization, let her know if you think her objectives seem reasonable, unrealistically high, or too low, and why you feel that way. If you fall into a pattern of always stretching them out no matter what they say, they'll sandbag the process.

Clarifying the desired objectives is just as important for your sake as for theirs. Management means converting resources into better results. How can you do that unless everyone is clear about what those results should look like?

The Playing Field, Parameter #4: Long-Term Results

Long-term objectives focus on 18 months to three years from now. If you and your team members don't look up from what is right in front of you, you will always just execute tactics. If you discuss with your team members the expected outcomes for the next three years, you cause them to think beyond the moment. They will start to ask questions such as, "What do we need to put in place in order to achieve those outcomes?" "Who do we need to influence?" and "What resources do we need in order to successfully implement those plans?" The long-term focus forces people to think strategically.

Evaluate whether your employees do things today that will generate the desired results three years from now. If all their activities focus on generating short-term results, you will never take your organization to a higher level. In reality, you will probably take your organization to a lower level because your good competitors will raise their performance bar year after year.

Summarizing The Playing Field

The first responsibility of management is to define The Playing Field. This means letting the employee know her behaviors and results are expected to fall within the desired values, strategy, short-term results, and long-term results. The more your employees understand these four parameters, the more freedom they have to operate.

A Manager's Second Responsibility: Coach

The word "coaching" is so overused it could almost include any activity. I've heard managers say, "I need to give that person some coaching." For them, coaching means yelling at the person for making a mistake or telling them exactly what to do in an upcoming situation. That's not what I mean by coaching. To me, coaching is about helping people think for themselves and decide how they will improve the desired results. If you do the thinking for your employees, you have wasted the opportunity to multiply yourself. Besides that, your team members may very well have better ideas than you do.

Coaching is really an act of leadership. The goal is to influence employees to think for themselves. You are not there to evaluate them or tell them what to do. To be an effective coach, you could use the approach described in Chapter 2 for Solution Leadership. The only difference in Chapter 2 and what I'm describing here is that in this chapter I'm talking about how you can influence people who report directly to you. The tools are the same, but the relationship might vary a bit. You coach by asking questions, providing analogies, offering suggestions, and so on.

Keep in mind this main point about coaching: you are trying to help the other person think for themselves rather than telling them how to handle the situation. Go back to my original analogy for this chapter of the referee telling the basketball coach to stay on the sidelines. When the player comes off the court, he or she is not playing in the game. That's when the basketball coach can ask questions, offer suggestions, and provide observations. The same is true in business. Meet with your employees away from the "game" itself. Don't give them advice during their interactions with customers or colleagues. Talk to them about the situation before and after the event happens.

Sample Coaching Questions

Here are questions you could use when you "coach" one of your direct reports:

- ◆ If you could change one thing about yourself that would have the greatest positive impact on driving better business results, what would it be and why did you select it? If another person came to you for advice on how they could make that change, what suggestions would you give?

- ◆ Imagine we are sitting here one year from today. As you look back over the past year, what achievements have you accomplished professionally? Why did you want these achievements? What strengths did you use to achieve these goals? What lessons from your past did use to make this happen?

- ◆ Tell me a success story from your past. What happened? How did you persevere? What did you learn? How could you apply those lessons toward achieving greater success today?

- ◆ What are three things you currently do that generate good results? How could you apply these activities in another area of your work to achieve better results in that area?

- ◆ What three things did you learn from other people in the past month either at home or at work? How could you apply those lessons in the next 30 days to achieve your goals?

What other questions might you ask? Notice the goal of each question is simply to cause the other person to pause, reflect on their situation, and direct their strengths toward achieving the desired outcome.

Keys to Effective Coaching

Here are five keys to keep in mind when coaching an employee:

1. Get your staff member to clarify the desired business outcome.

2. Cause this person to reflect on what she can do to achieve this desired outcome through questions, bold statements, or recent observations.

3. Offer suggestions and insights using a variety of techniques, including personal stories, famous stories, quotes, analogies, statistics, visual aids, and so on.

4. Get the other person to commit to her action plan.

5. Follow up consistently to identify what the other person did, what worked well for her, what did not work well, what lessons she learned, and what adjustments she will make in the future.

A Manager's Third Responsibility: Hold Your Employees Accountable

As the old saying goes, you get what you measure. Your employees will only take the Playing Field seriously if you hold them accountable to it. The first time an employee gets away with a behavior that does not gel with the stated values, your employees will doubt the importance of the values. The first time they get praise for achieving a great short-term outcome without sticking to the group's strategy, they will doubt the importance of the strategy. The first time they miss an important short-term objective and don't receive any kind of negative consequence, they will doubt you take results seriously.

If you don't hold your staff accountable for their behaviors and results, the Playing Field evaporates and you lose all credibility as a manager. Employees will behave in whatever way they want and achieve results to whatever degree they feel like. You won't be managing for success. You'll be fighting fires all day long.

You need to step in frequently and in many different ways to provide both positive and negative consequences to reinforce the importance of the desired behaviors and results. These kinds of interventions can range from a casual conversation in the hallway to the cash bonus incentive program.

A Manager's Fourth Responsibility: Stay off the Field

Staying off the field doesn't mean you don't have to follow the values for your group or the strategic direction for making decisions. Obviously, if you don't behave in the manner you expect from others, you dismantle the Playing Field very quickly. Keep in mind that this is an intangible field. It's only real if you make it real, and that starts with your behavior.

Staying off the field means setting aside your ego when you feel you can do the work better than anyone else. It means trusting your team members to do what you expect them to do and to deliver what you expect them to deliver. Staying off the field allows you to observe individual performance and make certain the efforts of the group still fit within the stated values and the strategic direction of the organization.

Every manager at every level in every organization has four responsibilities. They seem so basic at first glance, but fulfilling these responsibilities every day requires tremendous discipline and focus. Take care of your physical energy and your self-esteem. Those intangible factors will help you stay the course as you define the Playing Field, coach others, hold employees accountable, and stay off the field.

The Difference Between Mediocre and Magnificent Management

If management is such a straightforward activity, how do great managers separate themselves from average ones? It's a good question. In my consulting work, I get to observe executives and managers at different levels in many different industries several times a month. Over time, it has become very clear to me that the biggest difference between the great managers and the average ones is in the little things they do. This is not sexy or profound stuff. It won't make the cover of the *Wall Street Journal*. Essentially, the difference is quite subtle. But isn't that really the difference between a Norman Rockwell painting and the work of an average artist? What makes

Oprah Oprah? Isn't it really a lot of little things that separate her from others?

40 Subtle Management Tips

1.   Begin and end meetings on time.

This is a sign of respect for other people. Everyone in your organization is just as busy as you are. Don't mess with their calendars because of your needs. The whole operation will run more smoothly if you start and end meetings according to the schedule.

2.   Pass the praise, accept the blame.

You don't build esprit de corps by talking about building teamwork. You build it by repeated small acts. When things go well, shine the spotlight on specific individuals, specific groups, or the entire group, but never shine it on you. When things go poorly, be prepared to accept the blame. Just don't blame yourself so often people start to doubt your ability to function effectively. If you accept the blame for poor results a few times a year and explain your mistakes and your rationale for doing them, people will probably respect you more. Also, other people might step up and take responsibility for their portion of the poor results.

3.   Make the team the star.

If you want to build a team that continually generates better and more sustainable results, point out the collective strengths of the entire group. If your group excels at collaboration, point out how everyone's ideas contributed to the overall results. Make sure your praise, recognition, and incentives focus on the entire group's performance and not just the individual stars.

4.   Share the microphone.

I learned this one from one of my clients. Early on, he would be on stage, stand behind a podium, read a script, and go through PowerPoint slides. He then evolved to speaking from the floor with just a few notes and no slides. Then he realized the message would penetrate even further if he had audience members speak during his presentation. He would identify four to five key actions he wanted the audience members to do when they went back to the field, and he would have different audience members stand up during his presentation to tell the group how they implemented one of those five points. Suddenly, he became enormously effective in speaking to groups.

5. Leverage your strengths.

This is the tale of two managers. One was a creative font, and the other was the king of developing processes. The first one would latch onto one creative idea and sell it to his entire organization. That one idea would generate extraordinary results. The second one would constantly ask, "What is our process for dealing with situations like that?" Over time, he worked with his staff to develop a repeatable process for virtually every aspect of his organization. He also generated extraordinary results.

My point is, each individual was effective because he leveraged his strengths. If the creative manager had tried to develop processes that would outlive him, he would have become terribly frustrated and failed. He operated using intuition and spontaneity. The second manager would have been terribly frustrated with an environment where individuals didn't know their roles and responsibilities, and the various processes for different aspects of the business.

6. Leverage the strengths of each employee.

If you identify the greatest strengths in each of your employees and put them in a position to apply those strengths, you generate far better business results. One of my clients found a marketing manager who was average in marketing, but who had great talent and passion for analyzing numbers and explaining what they mean. The manager put the person in charge of business research, and he flourished.

7. Leverage the strengths of your group.

Groups develop unique strengths. It's hard to know a group's strengths until you've seen the members work together. Some groups are very good at steadily moving a number of small projects forward over a long period of time. Other groups are better at driving one big project forward for a brief period of time and then moving on to the next big thing. Identify what your current group is particularly good at doing, and put it in a position to succeed. Trying to force the group to meet your style can result in a terrible failure.

8. Recognize success early and often.

If you want to bring certain behaviors and results to life, congratulate people early and often when you see what you want. At a football clinic in the 1960s, John Madden asked Vince Lombardi what made a successful coach. Lombardi said the key was to know what you want the finished product to look like. He went on to explain that if you don't know exactly what you want the end product to look like, you might get the desired performance once and then lose it, because you didn't reinforce with your team that this is what you wanted.

9. Consistently raise your standards.

Delivering tomorrow what you delivered today is not success. That is being a status quo-er. Every quarter needs to be better than the one before it, both in terms of raising your standards and in terms of better clarifying the expected values, strategic direction, and results.

10. Stay true to yourself.

Few things irritate employees more than a manager who goes to a seminar and comes back with a whole new approach to growing the business. Don't be a "flavor of the month" manager, where your style and emphasis change constantly. Stick to your approach and let it evolve to a higher level over time.

11. Talk less, listen more.

I've yet to meet the manager who wouldn't benefit from genuinely listening more often. Almost nothing is more effective than asking a good open-ended question and listening patiently for the answer. In this manner, you show respect for your employees, allow them the opportunity to think for themselves, and learn a great deal from them.

12. Take evaluations seriously.

Either take evaluating your employees seriously or don't do it. I'll never forget the time when the principal at the high school where I was working told me I was an average teacher. When I asked what I needed to do to be an excellent teacher, he said I needed to stand on my desk and juggle balls like at a circus. I lost all respect for him that day. If you can't clearly explain what you mean by your evaluation, don't do it.

Another classic waste of time is when an employee fills out their own evaluation and their boss approves it. What in the world is this? The primary benefit of an evaluation is to formally reinforce where the employee is and is not operating on the Playing Field. By doing an effective evaluation, the manager helps the employee understand how to improve his or her performance.

13. Model humility.

Lou Holtz, the former football coach at Notre Dame, used to say, "Things are never quite as good as they seem, nor as bad as they seem, but somewhere in between reality lies." If you can remain humble when your team generates extraordinary results, they will be more likely to listen to you when results are poor.

14. Learn from your boss.

Every boss you have teaches you something. Some teach you valuable ideas and approaches, and others teach you how not to behave. Analyze each boss you've had and make a list of the qualities you want to incorporate and those you don't.

15. Make a very big deal about your Corporate Values.

The Corporate Values posted on the wall have no meaning unless you bring them to life. If you want the people in your organization to act consistent with the desired behaviors, make a very big deal about the stated values. Don't just read them at meetings, conduct an autopsy with the members of your group of how well they have behaved in accordance with the stated values. Go through each of them and ask the group for examples of where they have followed the values and where they have not.

16. Analyze results.

The real importance of results is not in having them, but in analyzing them. Regardless of whether the results are good or bad, you generate real value by asking how they were achieved. You can examine these activities and determine what worked well, what didn't work well, what lessons were learned, and what changes need to be made in the future. If you do this for every important result, your staff members will start to do it on their own.

17. Courageously push back your boss.

Your boss is not always right. You know that, I know that, and she knows that. The challenge is to effectively push back your boss and get her to reconsider her input and direction. If you do it on every issue, your boss will ignore you and avoid you. If you never do it, your boss will question what value you bring to the table. When you occasionally challenge your boss's thought process, keep it professional and objective. Say, "I would be glad to consider doing that, but help me to understand how that fits with our strategy." Or "It sounds good, but I'm not sure it's a higher priority activity than what we are working on right now. What do you think? Which item do you think we should take off our radar screen?" Or "I think that would be the wrong approach for our group to implement and here are the reasons I feel this way…." Be honest and direct.

18. Improve at least one thing about yourself each year.

The most effective executives I've worked with always look to improve at least one aspect of their management or leadership skills each year. The key is for you not to fall into the illusion of "improving leadership competencies." By that, I mean the infatuation some companies have with improving competencies in a vacuum. I've seen people get rated higher on some "leadership competency" even though their results suffered miserably. Skill development has to be a subset of accelerating results, not a substitute. Ask yourself, "What high priority business outcome is my group working to achieve this year? In what way am I going to improve myself to better help my team achieve that goal?" Notice, the result and the development are linked together.

19. Avoid arrogance.

An arrogant manager thinks he or she has all the answers. Being arrogant is living an illusion. You never have all the answers. Being arrogant stifles creative thinking from your group members and causes top talent to move away from you. An arrogant manager is the antithesis of the manager who generates significant, sustainable, and profitable growth.

20. Avoid polite dictatorships.

Polite dictators are a pain in the butt. These are the managers who smile as they continually explain why the employees are always wrong. They patronize their staff members in front of the group, but blow off all input and go their preset way behind closed doors. When I see a manager compliment an employee in front of an audience and ridicule the individual behind his or her back, I know I'm dealing with a polite dictator. Dictators make all the decisions for their people, which is not exactly the behavior that generates great thinking or great long-term results.

21. Learn from every employee.

This is one of the keys to continual growth. As a manager, you work in a learning laboratory every day. If you genuinely work to learn something from every employee, you constantly grow and gain more value to offer in the future. I've yet to work with a client from whom I didn't learn something.

22. Argue for the customer.

One client told me his job was to argue for the customer. I love that. Suddenly, every decision by a staff member goes through the filter of "What would the customer say about this?" In this way, you convert a person's subjective, emotional, and personal approach into a more objective, rational, and broad approach that is required to meet the needs of the customer.

23. Avoid position power.

As the manager, you need to make the final decisions on a host of issues, and, many times, your decisions will contradict the input you received from your team. That's okay, because everybody understands your responsibilities. When you tell someone to change his or her schedule because you want to go home early, you use your position power to an extreme. That is counterproductive to influencing others effectively. Remember, be firm on the important decisions, and humble in your day-to-day interactions.

24. Don't embarrass people.

As I said, the difference between a great manager and an average one is in the little things. A subtle aspect of great management is to avoid embarrassing people. Once I saw a staff member lose her cool during a rehearsal and become very demanding of her peers. The manager patiently waited until she was done. When the two of them spoke later, he said, "You probably weren't aware of how in-depth these rehearsals can get. Is there anything you think could make your performance better for tomorrow?" She apologized for losing her cool, said she was a little nervous about the next day's meeting, made a few adjustments, and gave a solid presentation.

25. Be prompt.

Again, this is about respecting other people. If you arrive late just because of your title, you lose the respect of your staff and you can kiss goodbye the idea of bringing the Playing Field to life.

26. Don't get too friendly with employees.

I was a head college soccer coach for the first five years after college graduation. Early on, someone gave me great advice: be friendly, but not too friendly, with your players. Relaxing with your staff can be very effective in building relationships and laying a foundation for future results. However, getting drunk in front of your staff doesn't exactly build trust or respect.

27. Don't swear.

This may sound a little preachy, but I've yet to see a manager swear frequently in front of their staff and be respected for it. I really think swearing is an old-school technique and needs to be left out. Showing emotion, getting upset, and being honest with your frustrations can be very effective, but using foul language on a regular basis is more embarrassing than effective.

28. Be yourself.

To this day, the best advice I've ever received was from Dennis Grace, my soccer coach in college. After college graduation, I worked at the summer soccer camps at Indiana University, which was the premier college soccer program in the nation. There were always All-Americans and professional players at these camps. Because I was "First-Team Bench Player" for four years in college, I tended to be a little bit in awe of these folks. Coach Grace said, "Dan, here's a piece of advice, and I hope you never forget it. Just let Dan be Dan." In other words, don't try to be someone that I'm not. I encourage you to follow this advice as well. Just be yourself, not your boss or anyone else. That way, people know what to expect from you in every situation.

29. Have the courage to go it alone.

If every one of your peers does the project a certain way and you don't believe in it, have the courage to generate results a different way. You might get fired, but your career goal is not to be a robot. Your organization needs people who try different approaches, otherwise how will they know what will and won't work? You may have the only group in the company focused on establishing values, strategy, and desired outcomes. That's fine. If you believe in doing these things, stay the course. Your group might be the only one calling customers to see how their experience with your company went. That's fine. Just stay focused on improving results in whatever way you think is most appropriate as long as it fits on the Playing Field.

30. Take good care of details.

Effective management includes focusing on the details. Is it clear who is responsible for the lighting at the big meeting? Does everyone know the timing of the different parts of the upcoming presentation? Does everyone know who is picking up whom at the airport? These are details. Nobody will even notice unless they are not taken care of. The great managers ask questions about the details.

31. Base your input on facts whenever possible.

If you tell your team they do a great job, have some facts to back that statement up. Instead of just saying the results are great, let them know how long it has been since these results were last achieved, or how much better they are than the best year in the company's history. Avoid vague, meaningless statements by providing some texture to why you said what you said.

32. Focus on behaviors, results, and strategic alignment.

Don't criticize people because their style is different from yours or because they handled the situation different than the way you would have. Instead, give them feedback in terms of the parameters of the Playing Field: their behaviors, their strategic alignment, and their results. That's what they should be held accountable for.

33. Be comfortable with ambiguity.

Management consists of a constant series of decisions. Questions run through a manager's mind all of the time, including, "Should I clarify the values one more time, or should I hold the individuals accountable right now?" "Should I provide more coaching, or should I fire this person?" and "Is it time for me to raise my standards, or should I give the group some space to relax?" While the activities of management are fairly straightforward, the execution requires constant flexibility in dealing with gray areas. Many times there is no "right" answer.

34. Schedule "my time."

Far too often, managers wear the "I'm very, very busy" button like the red badge of courage. They act like being busy is a great thing. Folks, it ain't. Schedule a one-hour block of time each week and call it "my time." During this hour, simply focus on one or two key issues you've been dealing with. Analyze the issue from multiple angles and write different approaches you could use to improve it. Then make a decision and develop an action plan. Keep this block of time as sacrosanct as you would a meeting with a key customer.

35. Clarify expectations early and often.

When a new manager takes over a group, they tend to say, "I'm just going to observe for a while before I make any decisions." There's an upside to this approach. However, because the employees don't know what is expected of them, they will continue to do what they've done in the recent past. Many times, the new manager will be disappointed with his or her employees because their behaviors are not what the manager was looking for. This is *not* the employees' fault.

Unless you clarify the Playing Field, you can't expect your employees to know what behaviors you consider effective. You can always start by explaining broad behavioral expectations and narrow them down as time moves forward. Many times I've heard comments such as, "I can't believe a person at that level would behave that way." We're all human, and unless you clarify what behaviors you're looking for, you probably won't get them.

36. Don't assume people know what to do or how to do it.

Don't make the mistake of assuming people know how to do certain activities. Every professional athlete I've ever met has told me the first thing his or her coach does is focus on the fundamentals. If professional athletes begin with the fundamentals, why should your employees be any different? Don't assume the engineer who turned in great performances for years is automatically going to know how to manage a cross-functional team. Just because he or she has the title doesn't mean they've mastered the skill. Provide these individuals with the training needed to succeed.

37. Avoid sarcasm and cynicism.

Family members sometimes get sarcastic with each other because they've known each other for years and they put their guard down for a while. The same thing happens with long-time peers in business situations. They relax with each other and become sarcastic. But when a manager gets sarcastic or cynical with their staff, all kinds of problems rise up. First, it makes the manager look less like a manager and more like a peer. Second, it sets the tone that sarcasm and cynicism are acceptable behaviors. Consequently, the level of sarcasm and cynicism rises in the organization.

38. Say no more often, and yes less often.

Managers, especially those who want to move up the corporate ladder, tend to take on way, way, way too many things. As they do so they become less effective and less likely to get promoted. If you really want to be effective, clarify the highest priority business outcome, decide what few things you will do to drive that outcome, and decide what you will stop doing so you can stay focused.

39. Don't be Mr. or Ms. Fix-It.

People get promoted to a management position because they did a great job in a particular role. Good scientists become scientific managers, good salespeople become sales managers, and good operations people become operations managers. Consequently, these managers know a great deal about what needs to be done to improve results. The easiest, and least effective, thing for them to do is to step in and solve the problem. They look like geniuses, everyone applauds them, and the work process continues. What's the problem? The problem is, they never learn to leverage their knowledge. They never get their employees to think for themselves. They never replicate themselves. They simply become a very highly paid staff member.

40. Keep the monkey on the other person's back.

Instead of stepping in and solving the problem, keep the monkey on the other person's back. Ask questions such as, "What do *you* think is the best way to resolve that issue?" "What would *you* recommend to someone else?" "If you were in my position, what would *you* do?" Cause them to pause and reflect on the situation. Then let them know you are available to discuss the issue, but they are responsible for implementing their decisions.

THE CORPORATE CATALYSTIC CONVERTER

☑ The four responsibilities of management.

Every manager at every level in every organization has four responsibilities: define the Playing Field, coach each direct report, hold people accountable, and stay off the field.

☑ The parameters of the Playing Field.

The Playing Field consists of the desired values, strategy, short-term results, and long-term results. Values are beliefs that determine behaviors. Strategy is a guideline for making decisions that defines an organization, or a part of an organization, and the direction it is heading. Short-term results are the expected outcomes for the next one month, three months, six months, and year. Long-term results are the expected outcomes over the next 18 months to three years.

☑ Every effective business strategy is a branding strategy.

A brand is the perception of value that a customer thinks they receive from an organization or a prospect thinks they would receive if they bought from that organization. Always work to enhance the value your organization offers and the image your organization projects of its ability to deliver that value.

☑ The difference between magnificent and mediocre management.

Small, subtle differences separate the great managers from the average ones. To be a great manager, always be conscious of how you interact with people and what you say. Greatness is in the details.

Recommended Resources for Corporate Catalysts

The Practice of Management by Peter Drucker (HarperCollins, 1954).

This is the first book ever written on management as a discipline. It is pure genius. There really was no reason for another book on management after this one. I encourage you to study it and determine how you can apply Drucker's ideas in your organization.

Good to Great: Why Some Companies Make the Leap and Others Don't by Jim Collins (HarperBusiness, 2001).

This is my favorite business book of all. Collins attacks many of the corporate fallacies that have been around forever. He also makes a compelling argument for focusing on a few clear concepts. This became an instant business classic and is quoted in corporations all over the world.

Gung Ho: Turn On the People in Any Organization by Ken Blanchard and Sheldon Bowles (William Morrow, 1998).

This is one of the few books in the "short business novels" genre that I recommend. It's effective because it clearly explains the concept of the Playing Field in a fairly unique fashion.

Top Management Strategy: What It Is and How to Make It Work by Benjamin Tregoe and John Zimmerman (Simon & Schuster, 1980).

This is one of the earliest and best books on strategy ever written. Tregoe and Zimmerman provide a clear and straightforward approach to analyzing any organization's situation and the possible directions they can go. The cornerstone of their approach is for the organization to clarify its driving force.

Chapter 5

BORING CONSISTENCY, CONSTANT INNOVATION

IF YOU WANT A SILVER BULLET for accelerating organizational performance, here you go: boring consistency, constant innovation. Stay relentlessly consistent within the defined purpose of your business and constantly find ways to add more value to your customers. This is not one or the other. You can't grow your business just by making decisions that fit within the purpose of your business and ignore adding more value to your customers. On the other hand, if you just find ways to add more value to customers without staying within the framework of your defined purpose, you dilute your brand beyond recognition. You have to do both.

Execution of this mindset requires:

+ Understanding why it's important to operate within the definition of your business and to constantly improve within that framework.

+ Knowing how to define the purpose of your business.

+ Screening decisions to ensure your activities really do fit within your definition.

♦ Converting opportunities to create more value for your customers.

Faculty Input From "Corporate Catalysts University"

In their powerful book, *Profit From the Core: Growth Strategy in an Era of Turbulence* (Harvard Business School Press, 2001), Chris Zook, head of Bain & Company's Worldwide Strategy Practice, and James Allen, wrote:

> We see a tendency for strong core businesses to lose momentum by virtue of premature abandonment, miscalculation, or overreaching in search of new growth. We define sustained growth as growth in terms of both revenues and profits over an extended period of time while total shareholder returns (share price and dividend reinvestment) exceed the cost of capital. In this book, we focus on a single theme: the extraordinary importance of creating a strong core business as a foundation for driving company growth.

In 1998, these two men set out on a research project to systematically study a 10-year database of more than 8,000 companies' growth histories. One of their most powerful findings was "the key to unlocking hidden sources of growth and profits is not to abandon the core business but to focus on it with renewed vigor and a new level of creativity." The implications of that statement are extraordinary. It means boring consistency can generate phenomenal results.

Models of "Boring Consistency, Constant Innovation"

This simple concept has been proven over and over by the world's greatest companies. Here are 10 examples:

Louis Vuitton

According to the March 22, 2004, issue of *BusinessWeek*, Louis Vuitton is the world's biggest and most profitable brand in the luxury goods industry. Its 2003 revenue was twice its nearest competitor and its operating margins were 15 percent higher than the next highest performer. How does a company that charges $1,000 for a handbag create such extraordinary customer loyalty and continue to grow at such a profitable pace?

First, it keeps the quality of its products at incredibly high levels. To test a handbag, an 8-pound weight is inserted and the bag is dropped over and over again for four days. Zippers are tested by having a machine open and shut them more than 5,000 times. A mechanized mannequin hand shakes a Vuitton charm bracelet to make sure none of the charms fall off.

Second, Louis Vuitton never drops its prices and items never go on sale. In 2003, prices rose 10 percent to 12 percent in the midst of a tough economy. Everyone who carries or wears a Louis Vuitton item makes a statement about their level of success. It's like throwing a Mercedes-Benz over your shoulder and carrying it around.

Third, the company constantly looks to improve the image and the details of its products. When luxury accessories became red-hot in the late 1990s, Louis Vuitton brought in designers who created a unique new look for its products that helped to propel sales.

Fourth, its marketing consistently sends the message of a high-end, luxury lifestyle. In one ad, beautiful supermodels are draped over Vuitton luggage against a gold-and-turquoise desert landscape.

Southwest Airlines

When you hear Southwest Airlines, what comes to mind? I've asked this question of my participants at well over a hundred seminars. The answers I hear the most often are "cheap, fun, and convenient." For more than 30 years, Southwest Airlines has stayed focused on delivering those three value-added items while constantly finding ways to get better at them. Their employees even share the jokes that worked well with customers.

Honda Motor Company

Customers of Honda know they will have few breakdowns, average costs, phenomenal quality, and extraordinary year-round service.

Honda constantly works to maintain reasonable costs and improve quality and service. One of its greatest assets is the high resale value of its cars.

Nokia

Among the best cell phones in the world and always getting better. Notice how the great brands are identified by as little as one sentence. According to *Fast Company* magazine (June 2004), Nokia controlled 12 percent of the global market for cell phones in the early 1990s and 38 percent by 2004. Frank Nuovo was brought on board as chief designer in the early 1990s and began to reposition the cell phone as fashion technology and a personal accessory. Even though his bosses didn't understand his thought process, they allowed him to completely redesign their cell phone into an item that appealed to different consumer groups. They remained fanatical about quality, and constantly innovated the design of their phone.

Berkshire Hathaway

Their purpose is to invest for the long term in extremely well-managed businesses that are fairly easy to understand. Warren Buffett, chairman of Berkshire Hathaway, admits his approach is boring, but he also says he feels his job is to tap dance to work, and lay on his back and paint the Sistine Chapel every day. The guy never lets up, but he also never falls for the trap of the illusionary quick buck. Remember when people called him a fool for not investing in the dot-com madness?

Wal-Mart

Wal-Mart provides the most merchandise at the lowest price of any retailer in the world, and the company has done it for more than 40 years. Wal-Mart truly democratized consumer goods, and it keeps offering more for less.

General Electric

It develops extraordinary management talent and applies it to a wide array of corporations. Some people argue that GE has no brand, but that's because these people are looking for an iconic product, service, or business model. That's not GE. GE is boringly consistent at developing management talent and constantly innovative in deploying these managers to a wide variety of businesses. In 2004, they returned to their creative roots by buying Vivendi Universal and Amersham, the British medical-imager.

FedEx

When you absolutely, positively need it delivered overnight. FedEx was fast from the very beginning, and has worked to get even faster.

Starbucks

In the January 26, 2004, issue of *Fortune*, Howard Schultz, chairman of Starbucks, said, "Starbucks has become what I call the third place. The first place is home. The second place is work. We are the place in between. It's a place to feel comfort. A place to feel safe. A place to feel like you belong." Starbucks is a perfect illustration of boring consistency and constant innovation. Its basic purpose has never changed from the days when the little-known store started to catch momentum in 1987, but if you wander through a Starbucks today you'll see a steady stream of improvements.

Ted Drewes Frozen Custard

Outside of St. Louis, few people know of Ted Drewes Frozen Custard, even though it was named one of the 10 best retail ice cream stores by *USA Today*. What's its secret? While there are only two locations, they have focused on providing the highest quality frozen desserts since 1928. No cakes, no cookies, no pies—just frozen custard. But every year they add a new concoction and find ways to make the customer experience better.

I used this relatively unknown example to make a point. You don't have to run an internationally known brand or even run an entire company in order to apply the concept of "boring consistency, constant innovation." You just have to clarify the purpose of your business or business unit, make sure your group stays boringly consistent within that purpose, and constantly search for ways to improve performance.

Case Study: Oprah Winfrey

Oprah Winfrey has generated significant, sustainable, and profitable growth for a long, long time. How did she do it? For more than 20 years, she focused on empowering women through a combination of intellectually and emotionally stimulating topics. Yet, she never stopped searching for ways to add more value to her audience, whether it was through her television show, the books she recommended, or her magazine. During a brief lapse in the mid-90s, she followed the trend of other talk shows with bizarre themes and deviant guests. However, she quickly moved back to her boringly consistent and constantly innovative focus on enriching women. When she did, she became more popular than ever.

Benefits of Operating Within Your Defined Purpose and Constantly Improving

Here are some of the benefits I believe any group can gain by staying consistent and constantly improving:

1. Increase customer loyalty.

The American Girl business has one of the most loyal customer bases in the world. Founded in 1986 by Pleasant Rowland as a company to educate and entertain girls, The American Girl business provides an extraordinary array of enriching experiences for girls. From the Bitty Baby to the extremely authentic and detailed American Girl Dolls to the books that explain the early history of the United States through stories about young girls to the American Girl stores in Chicago and New York City and much more, the American Girl business, which is an independent subsidiary of Mattel, sticks to its original purpose while constantly finding new ways to add value to girls. It's not uncommon for a 2-year-old girl to start with a Bitty Baby, receive additional clothes for this doll as gifts for the next several years, evolve to more dolls with more clothes and books to learn additional information about the dolls, and eventually become a 10-year-old who travels to the American Girl stores. Wouldn't you love to have that kind of customer loyalty in your business? The keys are to know your company's purpose, stick to it over the long term, and constantly create more value for your loyal customers.

2. Increase employee loyalty.

When people know they're part of something special, they don't want to leave. By staying focused and constantly getting better, your organization or group becomes an icon in the industry. People want to stay with a winner. In an article titled, "The Costco Way" by Stanley Holmes and Wendy Zellner (*BusinessWeek*, April 12, 2004), an old-fashioned approach for driving business results was brought to light. On the way to generating a 25 percent profit and 14 percent sales gain in the most recent quarter, Costco showed that you can take good care of your employees and still succeed in a very competitive environment. In a direct comparison with their nearest competitor, Costco paid more than 30 percent higher wages, provided more than 50 percent better health costs, covered 35 percent more of their employees' health plans, and gave nearly 90 percent better retirement benefits. By providing extraordinary support for its employees, Costco achieved significantly lower turnover and higher productivity. CEO James Sinegal said, "Paying your employees well is not only the right thing to do, but it makes for good business." Julie Molina, a 17-year Costco hourly worker said, "Employees are willing to do whatever it takes to get the job done." According to the authors, "Costco gets one of the most productive and loyal workforces in all of retailing. Only 6 percent of employees leave after one year. That saves tons." These loyal employees "constantly search for ways to repackage goods into bulk items, which reduces labor, speeds up Costco's just-in-time inventory and distribution system, and boosts sales per square foot."

3. Attract talent more easily.

By being known as the best in your field, you will find it much easier to hire talented people. That's the kind of organization every superstar wants to join. It's part of the reason why the best college athletic teams stay so good. The same is true for a great corporation or even a great department inside a corporation.

4. Develop subtle expertise.

By maintaining focus in a given field, you start to acquire subtle skills you otherwise would not learn. A neighbor of mine has a degree in mechanical engineering. He also has owned a local bar for more than 15 years. By constantly innovating, he learned how to make great pizza, and recently his bar was voted as having the best pizza in St. Louis. You generally don't get that information in a course on thermodynamics.

5. More quickly advance your business.

With sustained focus, you become more like a laser beam than a shotgun. You can seize appropriate opportunities faster than the competitors who dabble in many different fields. When Wal-Mart wanted to sell groceries, it instantly became the world's largest grocer. Dell, Inc., is a super-efficient distributor of manufactured items. When they wanted to expand into distributing electronic products beyond computers, they moved very, well, efficiently.

6. Save resources.

The discipline of staying focused saves an enormous amount of time, energy, and money from going down the drain.

7. Create greater camaraderie.

The turnover rate of employees, called Cast Members, at Disney World is low for the industry, even though the employees receive average pay. People from all over the world try to get a part there. Bottom line: people want the feeling of esprit de corps in their lives.

What other benefits do you see of staying boringly consistent and constantly innovative? Make your list as long as you can. Get the other members of your group to identify the benefits.

How to Define the Purpose of Your Business

You can clarify the purpose of your business, department, or group in the following manner:

1. Have members of your group finish any of these statements:
    "We are in the business of _____."
    "We are in the _____ business."

"The purpose of our business is to ____."
"The reason our customers buy from us is ____."

2. Break them into smaller groups of four to six people. Have each person read his or her statement. Then have the members of the small group discuss their ideas and narrow them to a single statement summarizing the purpose of the business, department, or group from their perspective.

3. Have everyone hear what each of the small groups came up with. Then ask for a volunteer to take a stab at summarizing what has been said into a rough draft of a purpose statement.

Corporate Catalyst Tip #5:
Don't Use the Words "Vision" and "Mission"

Avoid using the words "mission" and "vision." I've found many businesspeople are burned out on these words. As soon as they hear them, they check out of the discussion by saying, "We did that years ago. It was a waste of time." I suggest you keep it conversational with questions such as, "So, why would anybody buy from us?" "How are we really different than the competition?" "What's the point of our business?" "Why does our business exist anyway?" and "If we were really successful, what would that success look like?" Don't turn this into the nightmare some companies endure when they invest six months developing a purpose statement that gets ignored anyway. A couple of sessions should suffice. Clarify the purpose and get on with being boringly consistent.

---

4. Gain input from all of the participants about what they think should stay in the rough draft, what should come out, and what should be added to it. The final statement of purpose doesn't have to be perfect, but it does have to gain a high level of consensus.

5. In addition to clarifying the purpose from an internal perspective, interview a dozen customers. I'm not talking about running a focus group. I mean walk up to a customer or call them on the phone and have a real-life conversation. Ask questions such as, "What do we do that you really appreciate?" "What could we do that would add a lot more value to you?" and "How would you define the purpose of our business?"

6. Compare the answers your group came up with to the comments from your customers. Make any final adjustments to your defined purpose as a business so it represents reality.

The Three Great Acceleration Tools

I believe the three most powerful tools for accelerating critical business outcomes are *clarity*, *simplicity*, and *sustained focus*.

- Clarify the purpose of your business or group, clarify the highest priority outcomes to be achieved, and clarify what could be done to achieve them. Make the purpose as clear as possible. Make it so clear that a complete stranger can understand it on the first attempt.

- Simplify everything. Simplify the HPOs to the top two or three so every employee understands them. Simplify the list of what needs to be done to the three activities that will have the greatest positive impact on achieving each desired outcome.

- Stay relentlessly focused over the long term. Don't go off on tangents. Don't lose your enthusiasm for the purpose or the outcome. Stay focused.

A large percentage of the executives and managers I've encountered work extensive hours and do a dozen things simultaneously. Their mantra is "I'm busy," and they really mean it. Not necessarily effective, but most definitely busy. As their executive coach, I encourage them to define their boundaries in terms of how much time they give to their professional life and narrow their focus in terms of what they are trying to achieve. By working within tighter parameters, they invariably achieve better results in the areas that matter the most. This shift is displayed in Figure 5.1.

Clarity, Simplicity, and Focus

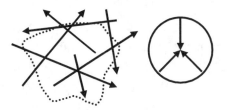

Figure 5.1

Rather than doing seven activities that attempt to generate five different outcomes, narrow your focus to the three things that will have the greatest positive impact on generating your highest priority business outcome. Clarify, simplify, and sustain your focus. That's really boring and really effective.

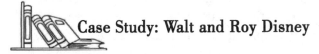

Case Study: Walt and Roy Disney

The late 1940s was not a good time for The Walt Disney Company. As the rest of the country surged forward, The Walt Disney Company slumped backward.

In 1937, The Disney Company made the film, *Snow White and the Seven Dwarfs*, which was the first full-length animated film. People called it "Disney's Folly" and said Walt Disney was an idiot. They said he was going to ruin his business. The film became the highest grossing film of that time. It brought in more than $6 million, and with that money, Walt Disney built the Disney Animation Studios. In 1941, The Disney Company came out with the film *Dumbo*, which was another smash hit. These were the go-go days for the company.

In December 1941, Pearl Harbor was attacked and the world changed. The Disney Animation Studios were converted into war studios, where they made animated films for the military until the end of the war in 1945. From 1945 to 1949 the company floundered. In late

1949, Walt and Roy Disney sat down to have a brotherly discussion. In other words, they had a big fat fight, which went something like this:

Roy said, "Walt, we have got to make more money in every part of our business."

Walt replied, "We have artistic standards to uphold."

Roy came back with, "Walt, if we don't start making more money, we aren't going to have any standards to worry about."

Walt defiantly replied, "If we're not going to do it right, then let's get out of this business. Let's just liquidate everything and sell off our assets."

Roy, completely frustrated, said, "Walt, what do you want to do? What are we trying to become?"

In a moment of extraordinary genius, Walt responded, "Our purpose is to provide quality family entertainment. Our job is to entertain all members of the family."

In that moment, Walt and Roy Disney changed business forever, because from that point forward, businesses didn't just focus on selling products and services, they focused on building a brand. Under the umbrella of "quality family entertainment," The Disney Company started to add an array of new items, including two television shows, *The Mickey Mouse Club* and *Disneyland*; a new theme park, Disneyland; and live action films and other TV shows such as *Davy Crockett* and *Zorro*. Then the magic started to happen.

People would watch *The Mickey Mouse Club* and learn about the new theme park being built and the new films coming out. They would go see the animated and live action films and learn more about the Mouseketeers and the new theme park. When they went to Disneyland, they rode on rides that featured the characters from the animated films. Everything promoted everything else. From 1950 to 1959, The Walt Disney Company's revenues grew by 800 percent and the profits grew by 600 percent. This was no corporate start-up. In 1950, the company was 28 years old.

This era of excellence, which really lasted until Walt's death in 1966, is an extraordinary example of "boring consistency, constant innovation." Even on his deathbed, Walt tried to raise the bar by talking about the next theme park, Disney World. Why can't you be the Walt Disney in your organization? Ultimately, it's about being a corporate catalyst. (Source: *The Magic Kingdom: Walt Disney and the American Way of Life* by Steven Watts, Houghton Mifflin, 1997)

The Decision Filter

The most frequent question I hear regarding the topic of staying focused is, "How do I determine what to do and what not to do?" Unfortunately, there's no cookie-cutter way to screen an idea, but here's five suggestions.

1. Have to get two yes votes.

Within a group, any decision requires at least two people to vote yes in order to gain approval for moving forward. This seemingly small screen can keep one person from going off on a completely crazy idea.

2. Read first, reflect second, decide third.

Read over the purpose of your business several times and ask if the idea really fits within the framework of your business. If it does, consider moving forward. If it doesn't, no matter how much "easy" money can be made on the idea, don't do it.

3. Would you recommend the action if you were in charge?

Ask yourself if you would do it if you were the CEO of the company. This exercise forces you to look beyond just your group to your whole organization and how this decision impacts customers and employees. It also provides great practice in preparing you for future roles and responsibilities.

4. Consider your options.

Make a list of as many possible alternatives as you can generate. Then place this idea next to each of the options and see if it still shines through the pack.

5. If it's not critical, don't do it.

Challenge yourself repeatedly with the question, "Is this activity critical to the success of the project?" If it's not, then at least temporarily put it to the side. Keep filtering your possible activities until you get down to the critical few. It's far easier to jump into action than it is to assess your alternatives. However, a little more assessment can save you a great deal of time, energy, and money over the long term.

Faculty Input From "Corporate Catalysts University"

The real genius of Jim Collins, author of *Built to Last* and *Good to Great*, is his ability to craft a powerful statement in very few words. Over the years, his contributions to the business vocabulary have included "Level 5 Leadership," "First Who, Then What," "BHAGs: big, hairy, audacious goals," "Clock Building, Not Time Telling," and "Get the right people on the bus, put them in the right seats and get the wrong people off the bus." In his book, *Built to Last* (HarperBusiness, 1994), he and coauthor, Jerry Porras, coined another brilliant phrase, "preserve the core/stimulate progress." That book was all about "boring consistency, constant innovation."

Collins and Porras wrote, "It is absolutely essential to not confuse core ideology (core values and purpose) with culture, strategy, tactics, operations, policies, or other noncore practices. Over time, cultural norms must change; strategy must change; administrative policies must change; organization structure must change; reward systems must change. Ultimately, the only thing a company should not change over time is its core ideology."

Innovation: How to Systematically Raise the Bar

Is innovativeness a trait a person is born with? Nope. Innovation is one of the critical skills for corporate catalysts, and because it's a skill, it can be developed by anyone. Innovation is a process; inspiration is an event. Innovation consists of step-by-step approaches for identifying ways to add more value to customers. Inspiration is an idea that comes to you in the middle of the night or while you're driving or when you're taking a shower. An inspirational idea can be very useful for driving better results, but innovation is something you can count on consistently.

By understanding various processes of innovation, the corporate catalyst can guide a group to develop breakthrough actions they otherwise would never have considered. The key to successful innovation is to make sure you're innovating within the defined purpose of the business. In this manner, you maintain the sustainable part of SSPG.

Methods of Innovation

Here are four approaches to generate more value for customers:

Innovation Method #1: The CAT Method

The old adage that change is constant turns out to be a very good thing. This is my favorite innovative approach because it converts the constant changes in organizations, industries, and marketplaces into a steady flow of value-added opportunities. The CAT Method is based on ideas from two terrific books, *Innovation and Entrepreneurship* by Peter Drucker (Harper & Row, 1985) and *The Innovation Formula* by Michel Robert and Alan Weiss (Harper & Row, 1988).

CAT stands for:

- **C**larify the change.
- **A**nticipate the opportunity created by that change.
- **T**arget a specific product or service to meet the customer's new need or desire.

1. Make a list of changes that have occurred in your organization, your industry, or society in general over the past 24 months. These changes could fall under any of the following categories: unexpected successes, unexpected failures, changes in technology, changes in demographics, unexpected events or changes in perception.

2. For each of these changes, answer the question: what opportunity does this change create for us to add more value to our customers?

3. Examine each of these opportunities and answer the question: what product or service could we provide to leverage this opportunity into adding more value to our customers?

A famous example of The CAT Method is the story shared earlier about The Walt Disney Company in the 1950s. The post–World War II era generated enormous changes in American society. People had more leisure time, televisions, cars, and disposable income than at any previous point in history. They needed more entertainment options at a greater frequency. Walt Disney saw these opportunities. He created Disneyland, the theme park, to meet the new desire to travel for vacations. He created the television programs to meet the need for daily and weekly entertainment.

When music albums fell way to compact discs, a new opportunity was created in terms of manufacturing hard plastic containers for the fragile CDs. In the 1970s, when both parents started working outside of the home more often, an opportunity was created for frozen dinners. In the 1990s, the accessibility of knowledge and data transfer via the Internet created opportunities for virtual retail businesses such as Amazon and Borders.com.

The CAT Method converts the steady flow of changes you encounter every day into potential opportunities to grow your business.

Innovation Method #2: The creative process

This concept emerged for me from a really solid book called *Jamming: The Art and Discipline of Business Creativity* by John Kao (HarperBusiness, 1996). In this approach, you take your most important issue, turn it into a value-driven question, answer the question from a variety of perspectives, and develop new approaches to old problems. Here are the actual steps:

1. Include the decision-makers.

Unless the decision-makers are in on the ground floor, they probably won't see the value of the ideas the group generated. Human nature seems to cause people to poke holes in an idea if they did not help develop it. In some cases, you can do this process by yourself. In issues relevant to a large group, be sure to bring the key players in from the beginning.

2. Get the right environment.

Find a place away from your office where you can clear your mind and think. Find a space where you and the members of your group won't be interrupted. Take your group off-site, but not somewhere so nice or so pathetic they get distracted by the surroundings.

3. Focus on one issue at a time.

You can't generate new ideas when you focus on multiple issues simultaneously. When that happens, you revert to fighting fires and executing tactics. The key is to select only one issue on which to concentrate. By doing this, you gather all of your group's energy and mental resources and direct them toward the issue.

4. Turn the issue into a clear, specific, and value-driven question.

Every issue has a wide variety of perspectives. Say, for example, your issue is "sales." You might be interested in growing sales: growing sales with a specific client, growing sales with a broader client base, maintaining sales while reducing costs, growing sales for a specific niche market, or maintaining sales while working fewer hours. The single issue could have multiple meanings. The key is to ask a clear, specific, and value-driven question. Instead of asking, "How are things going with our sales team?" ask, "If we could change or improve one thing about the way we train and develop our sales force that would have the greatest positive impact on retaining customers, what would it be and why did you select it?"

5. Remove doubts.

Before trying to answer your question, identify all of your group's doubts regarding this topic. Until the group acknowledges and removes their doubts, you will have a limited chance of generating any breakthrough concepts. Write down a list of all the reasons why people think the group cannot successfully address this issue. Then take each doubt and complete this statement: "We will overcome this doubt by _____."

If you come down to a few doubts your group just can't figure out a way to resolve, identify the greatest doubt and turn it into your clear, specific, and value-driven question.

6. Clear away the mental clutter.

Get rid of the stuff that keeps people from thinking clearly. One way to do it is to consciously daydream. Have everyone in your group recall a favorite time in their life. Get them to focus on what they see for 30 seconds. Then have them focus on what they hear. Let it sink in. Finally, ask them to concentrate on what they feel at that moment.

The goal is for everyone to be totally immersed in the memory of a great experience. After two minutes, snap your fingers and bring everyone directly back to the value-driven question.

I've done that exercise with hundreds of people, and it never ceases to amaze me how quickly and vividly they can recall a situation that happened 30 years ago. The goal is to mentally let go of your to-do list and your concerns of the moment. Free your mind to think clearly. You will come back to the question ready to concentrate on the issue at hand.

7. Rotate the crops.

When a farmer plants the same crop on the same plot of land year after year, the nutrients in the soil begin to wear out and the land becomes less productive. The same thing happens when you examine the same problem from the same perspective over and over again. Eventually, you run out of new ideas for improving the situation.

It is important to view the issue from a variety of perspectives. For example, have different group members answer the specific, value-driven question from the perspective of the corporate president, a mid-level manager, an extremely loyal customer, a very difficult customer, a competitor, a salesperson with 20 years experience, a new sales person, an operations manager, and a marketing manager. Make a list of all the answers your group comes up with.

8. Combine ideas together.

Sometimes the most powerful breakthroughs happen when you combine two or more ideas to generate an even better idea. Have your group look for connections between their ideas and write down any ideas that emerge from these combinations. By doing this over and over again, you generate new approaches to old issues.

9. Select the best idea and take action.

Take a look at your list of ideas and select what you consider to be the best answer. You can analyze your ideas in a number of ways: efficiency versus effectiveness, cost versus benefit, impact to customers versus impact to employees, and so on. The key is to make a decision. The only way to learn what will or will not work is to try an idea.

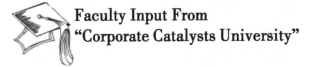

Faculty Input From
"Corporate Catalysts University"

Roy Spence, cofounder and president of GSD&M, is widely recognized as an innovator in the advertising industry and has been featured in the pages of *Fortune, Esquire, The Wall Street Journal, The New York Times,* and *USA Today.* Just in case you've never heard of GSD&M, it has been the advertising agency for Southwest Airlines for more than 20 years and represents some of the country's most-respected brands. Its client list includes Wal-Mart, DreamWorks, the PGA Tour, Chili's, Fannie Mae, SBC Communications, and a number of other companies that demonstrate the concept of "boring consistency, constant innovation."

Spence believes ideas are the currency of the 21st century. Also, in a speech to *Fast Company* magazine in 2004, Spence said, "In the 1990s we saw the rising tide. The changing tides test the strength of your anchor and the power of your purpose. If everyone's selling the same thing, what's going to be the tie-breaker? The first question we have when we do purpose-based branding is, 'What business are you in?'"

GSD&M focuses on helping companies constantly innovate within the framework of the defined purpose of their business, and their track record of success has been pretty phenomenal.

Innovation Method #3: Find matching definitions

Sometimes the best ideas for growing your business come from organizations completely outside your industry. Don't just use your peers or your competition as benchmarks for best practices. They may very well be using you for the same purpose, which could create an endless loop of parity. Reach out to other industries and find organizations sharing a definition with your organization.

Here's an example of this innovation process and how a grocery store might complete each step:

1. Define your organization by completing the following statement in as many different ways as you can: "We are a place _____."

ABC Groceries & More is a place _____

- where people come to get away from home and work.
- to load up for another week's onslaught.
- for all members of the family.
- that provides multiple forms of entertainment.
- where kids ride in carts.

2. Identify organizations that share one of these definitions.

- where people come to get away from home and work—a movie theatre.
- to load up for another week's onslaught—an army refueling its supplies.
- for all members of the family—family reunion.
- that provides multiple forms of entertainment—Las Vegas.
- where kids ride in carts—bumper cars in an amusement park.

3. Identify what each of these organizations does really well.

A movie theatre provides time before the film starts for people to buy popcorn, and the film creates a fantasy where viewers feel they have left their own world.

When an army refuels its supplies, the soldiers wear distinctive uniforms and stay ready for the enemy.

At a family reunion, everyone wears a nametag, everyone uses the other person's first name, and people are excited to be together.

In Las Vegas, there are bright flashing lights, there are many different games going on at the same time, the fun goes 24 hours a day, and customers don't know the time of day.

When they ride bumper cars in an amusement park, kids get to be loud and violent and scream and crash into each other, and their parents laugh while it's happening.

4. Decide how you can apply some of the ideas from the other organizations to your situation.

Using the movie theater example, give the customer a free bag of popcorn and a brightly colored sheet of paper describing where the different items are in the store just like the sign describing where the different films are showing. Have your employees wear vests and say things such as, "Now showing in Aisle 4 is 'Return of the Vegetables.'"

Using the army refueling supplies as an example, give any parent who comes into the grocery store with two or more children under the age of 5 an army fatigue jacket to wear in the store. This signifies that they may need special help while they are battling the environment.

Using the family reunion model, have some of your employees go up to customers when they walk into the store, ask for their first name, write it on a nametag, and hand it back to them. As the customers walk through the store, have the other employees greet them by name.

Using Las Vegas as the example, have a different colored light shining over every section of the store. Spread different types of games, including slot machines and roulette wheels, throughout the store. For 50 cents, customers can play these games and win points toward purchasing groceries.

Using bumper cars as the example, set up one specific aisle for "bumper activities," where children under 6 years old wear rubber helmets, get in carts that have rubber padding around them, and race each other up and down the aisle. When they crash into each other, rubber cans fall off the shelves and scatter all over.

5. Once you've generated a number of ideas, step back and see if you can develop any better ideas by combining two or more of these.

With the grocery store, you might end up with something like this scenario: When the customer walks in, an employee hands him or her a Bingo card, coins for the slot machines, a full-color written and visual description of where items are in the store, and army fatigues if they have children under the age of 5. Have entertainers dispersed throughout the store to bring life to a dull experience. Have clowns for the children, artists and magicians at every other aisle to perform for the customers waiting in line, and all of your employees dressed in bright colors. Play Bingo every 20 minutes. When customers leave the store, give them a schedule of "Upcoming Special Events," such as "Monster Bingo Night," different local musical groups, bumper car championships, and "The Shop 'Til You Drop" contest. Get customers talking about your store as providing memorable experiences and not just as a place to buy groceries.

Innovation Method #4: Be with the customer

Perhaps the fastest way to find good ideas is to talk directly with your customers. They know what does and doesn't work. Turn your group into an "Innovation Team" and have them use these four phases to develop more value for your customers:

Phase One

In order to gather valuable customer feedback, know what you want feedback on. Make sure this is clear to all members of the Innovation Team. You uncover tremendously valuable information by knowing what to ask questions about.

Phase Two

After you select the product, service, or customer experience you want feedback on, the Innovation Team invests the necessary time and energy to spend time with people who actually purchase and use it. They ask a few open-ended questions and see where the conversation goes. They need to be flexible in asking follow-up questions to dig deeper into what the customer wants. Get your Innovation Team members to as many customers as you can in a reasonable amount of time. Encourage them to have clear, specific, and value-driven conversations revolving around the one specific product, service, or customer experience you're investigating. If your team gets your customers to feel their input really matters, they will more likely open up and share their ideas.

Phase Three

After your group has met with customers, bring all of the Innovation Team members together to share their discoveries. Provide each member with the opportunity to speak to the rest of the group and share every tidbit of information they gathered. As each person speaks, the other members jot down ideas. After each speaker, the other members share the ideas that struck them while they listened. After everyone has spoken, the leaders of the Innovation Team analyze the input and gather it under four or five themes.

Phase Four

Divide the Innovation Team into Theme Teams, one per theme. The responsibility of each Theme Team is to develop new ideas for improving their particular area of the product, service, or customer experience they've been assigned. Then all of the Theme Teams come together for a large group discussion. Each Theme Team explains its ideas for improving its particular aspect, and the other members of the group provide feedback until all ideas on a particular theme have been exhausted. Once all the themes have been covered, each member of the Innovation Team votes on the ideas he or she wants included in the final revision. After the voting is finished, the final tallies indicate the opportunities for improvement the group will move forward with. (*Source: The Art of Innovation: Lessons in Creativity from IDEO, America's Leading Design Firm* by Tom Kelley with Jonathan Littman, Currency/Doubleday, 2001)

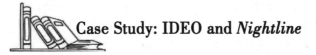 **Case Study: IDEO and** *Nightline*

In 1999, the extraordinarily innovative design company IDEO took on a challenge from the television show *Nightline*. *Nightline* gave them a product, a grocery store shopping cart, to improve within five days. Watching this show was the moment when I really learned the value of generating ideas by being with the customer. (You can watch this video about IDEO by calling 1-800-CALL-ABC. The product code is N990713-01.)

First, the group of 15 to 20 designers went to local grocery stores to talk with consumers and employees about the shopping carts. They heard the customers' point of view on every aspect of the shopping cart, including safety, convenience, children riding in it, the value of the cart itself, and many others.

The design team reconvened two days later. Each person shared his or her insights about the shopping cart. Meanwhile, other members jotted down their notes. After every presentation, other team members shared their thoughts.

In the end, the group divided the overall input into four major themes and assigned group members to each theme. These smaller groups had one day to develop their suggestions for improvement and to present them to the large group. After each presentation, the large group discussed what they heard, offered additional advice, made adjustments, and voted on what parts to keep. Then the best of the best ideas from the four presentations were merged into a final design.

At this point, the group turned the design over to the prototype team. These master craftspeople began to assemble a completely different type of shopping cart with five plastic removable cartons, wheels that turned 90 degrees, a special seat with working space for children, and many other innovations.

It was a beautiful example of increasing the value to customers by looking at a product from the customer's point of view.

The Importance of Evaluating Ideas

Of course, just accumulating ideas does not accelerate your desired outcomes. You need to evaluate those ideas and find the ones that matter most. The primary concept to keep in mind in evaluating ideas is the impact they could have on your most important desired outcomes. Ideas should never be implemented simply because of their source, that is, the head of the group came up with it or the group is excited to try it. Conduct a preliminary evaluation of each idea by answering these two questions:

1. "Does it fit within the purpose of our business?"
2. "Does it leverage the strengths of the people in our organization?"

If it passes through these filters, test market the idea on a small scale. See if it delivers the desired impact. Identify what works well and what does not work well. Clarify the lessons you learned during the test market phase and apply those lessons as you move into applying the idea on a larger scale.

Sample of Evaluating and Comparing Three Ideas

Here is another process you could use to evaluate and compare ideas for adding more value to customers. (Source: *The Innovation Formula* mentioned earlier in this chapter.)

1.   Decide which of your organization's results you want improved.

Say your group wants to improve results in the following areas:

- Market Share.
- Comparable Sales.
- Cash Flow.
- Retention of Top Performing Employees (TPEs).
- Transaction Counts.
- Dollar Value of Average Transaction.

2.   Decide the relative value of each outcome.

You do this by deciding how much each outcome is worth compared to the other outcomes. Within this example, say your group assigned the following weights:

- Market Share × 1.
- Comparable Sales × 3.
- Cash Flow × 3.
- Retention of Top Performing Employees × 2.
- Transaction Counts × 2.
- Dollar Value of Average Transaction × 2

3.   Estimate the potential impact of each idea.

On a scale of 1 to 10, with 10 being the highest impact, estimate the impact you believe each idea could have on each of the desired outcomes. You can use as much in-depth research or gut feeling as you want in determining the numerical value. For the sake of this example, say your team assigned the following numbers to describe what they believe the impact of each idea will be on each outcome.

Impact Scores

	Idea 1	Idea 2	Idea 3
Market Share	8	7	9
Comparable Sales	5	9	7
Cash Flow	9	3	7
Retention of TPEs	7	2	6
Transaction Counts	5	9	7
Dollar Value of Average Transaction	9	9	8

4. Multiply the impact score by its relative weight for each outcome to see the objective value of each idea.

Here is a comparison of the objective value of the three ideas in our example:

	Idea 1	Idea 2	Idea 3
Market Share	$8 \times 1 = 8$	$7 \times 1 = 7$	$9 \times 1 = 9$
Comparable Sales	$5 \times 3 = 15$	$9 \times 3 = 27$	$7 \times 3 = 21$
Cash Flow	$9 \times 3 = 27$	$3 \times 3 = 9$	$7 \times 3 = 21$
Retention of TPEs	$7 \times 2 = 14$	$2 \times 2 = 4$	$6 \times 2 = 12$
Transaction Counts	$5 \times 2 = 10$	$9 \times 2 = 18$	$7 \times 2 = 14$
Dollar Value of Average Transaction	$9 \times 2 = 18$	$9 \times 2 = 18$	$8 \times 2 = 16$
Objective Value of Each Idea	92	83	93

Now, the hard part. You have to trust the process. Through this process, you identified Idea #3 as the best idea for generating your desired outcomes. Notice that Idea #2 has the greatest potential impact on Comparable Sales, Transaction Counts, and Dollar Value of Average Transaction. However, its overall objective value is significantly outpaced by Idea #3. In the emotion of a meeting, you may jump at Idea #2 without realizing you're sacrificing an even better idea.

THE CORPORATE CATALYSTIC CONVERTER

☑ Continually work to clarify the purpose of your business.

Regardless of your level of responsibility, it is crucially important for you and your group to understand why your business exists. How can you remain consistent with something unless you understand it?

☑ Filter every decision and every activity in your group through this question: "Does this support the purpose of our business?"

If it doesn't, then do everything possible to stop it.

☑ Challenge other people in your company to stop doing things that don't support the purpose of your business.

Explain to them the negative impact these activities can have on the brand over the long term. Be patient and guide them through the discussion by asking open-ended questions.

☑ Within this disciplined approach, constantly search for ways to add more value to your customers.

Be sure your innovations focus on your customers and not just on internal issues, otherwise you'll end up with a great place to work and no customers, which is not really that great after all.

☑ Be systematic about leveraging opportunities to create more value.

Don't just wait for the great inspiration that comes to you in the middle of the night. By being systematic, you will find great ideas come to you more often.

Recommended Resources for Corporate Catalysts

In addition to all of the books I've mentioned in this chapter, here are three more:

The Tipping Point: How Little Things Can Make a Big Difference by Malcolm Gladwell (Little, Brown & Company, 2000).

This is a very unique book that explains how trends are created. In particular, Gladwell talks about "The Stickiness Factor," which is the single most important reason why certain things, ideas, or diseases take off until they reach their tipping point and suddenly become epidemics. Your stickiness factor is the purpose of your group or organization. As you stay with it and constantly improve, you increase your stickiness factor.

The Discipline of Market Leaders by Michael Treacy and Fred Wiersema (Perseus Books, 1995).

Another real gem, this book explains the importance of defining and operating within a clear strategy for growing your business. The authors provide three alternative strategies: product excellence, operational excellence, and customer intimacy. They explain how you can separate yourself from the pack and become a market leader by staying boringly consistent within your strategy and constantly innovating.

Managing for Results by Peter Drucker (HarperPerennial, 1964).

This was the first book ever written on business strategy, and my personal favorite. The examples are obviously dated, but the input is at least as relevant today as it was in 1964.

Chapter 6

"It's the Relationship, Stupid"

During the 1992 U.S. presidential campaign, James Carville gave Bill Clinton four pearls of wisdom when he said, "It's the economy, stupid." With that concept as his platform, Bill Clinton managed a narrow victory over incumbent George Bush. No matter what question he was asked, Clinton quickly redirected the conversation to how he would jump-start a flailing U.S. economic situation. All aspiring corporate catalysts can apply these four similar pearls of wisdom: "It's the relationship, stupid."

Every Business Is a Relationship Business

Every one of my clients has told me his or her business is unique. No matter what industry my clients operate in, they say, "Dan, this group is a tough crowd. They have very different problems than any other industry you've worked in. Our company has a very unique culture." On the one hand, they're absolutely right. Every corporate culture *is* unique. On the other hand, they don't realize how much they have in common with other businesses. Primarily, every business is a relationship business. Here are some examples:

➢ Biotech

Before you think biotech companies major in genes and minor in cells, let me remind you that no biotech company lasts for long without healthy relationships between the scientists, founders, venture capitalists, suppliers, and a host of adjacent organizations.

➢ Retail Store

Whether it's about shoes, sweaters, or purses, the real business of retail is a satisfied customer who gets what they want at a reasonable price. You can fool the customer once or twice, but once the relationship is gone, so are the sales.

➢ Computer Manufacturer

Whether you manufacture computers or cars doesn't really matter. What does matter is whether you understand the buyers' needs and consistently meet those needs. In other words, do you strengthen or weaken the relationship each day?

➢ Quick-Service Restaurant

Smiles count for a lot in this industry. A lack of friendliness in a 90-second transaction hurts the bottom line as much as a rude flight attendant does in a 90-minute flight.

➢ Financial Services Firm

If you work in this industry or any number of other professional service firms, ask yourself these three questions:

1. Do I really know the person to whom I'm selling?
2. Do I really know what I'm selling?
3. Do the two really make for a good match?

If the answer is consistently yes to all three questions, you will build long-term business relationships.

➢ Insurance Agency

Odds are you don't see your insurance agent very often, but if he or she doesn't respond to your occasional need quickly and accurately, the relationship won't last much longer.

➢ Construction Business

It may look like a business of bulldozers, but the relationships between contractors and subcontractors, clients, government officials, and suppliers represent the differentiating factors in this industry. Equally critical are the relationships between the senior-level executives, project managers, supervisors, foremen, estimators, and so on.

How to Build a Business Relationship

You build business relationships the same way you build personal relationships:

1. **Work to understand your customer.**

Understand the customer's highest priority outcomes. If you work one-on-one with customers, focus on the individual's HPOs. If you deliver value to thousands of customers simultaneously, work to understand the needs of different types of customers. You may have nine different types of customers, and you need to understand what matters to each type.

2. **Clarify what your customers can expect from you.**

Communicate clearly to your customers what they can realistically expect to receive from your organization. If you can't deliver it, don't create that expectation. If your ability to deliver a certain expectation weakens, let your customers know as soon as possible. If you fail to do this, your relationship will sour quickly. In 2004, the Royal Dutch/Shell Company moved from one set of problems to another because it did not quickly communicate that estimated reserves were, well, *over*estimated for a long time.

3. **Deliver, at minimum, what is expected of you.**

Before you attempt to create additional value for customers, be sure to deliver what is expected of you. If your customers expect fast and friendly service, don't think a new product offering will overcome the problems of slow and rude service.

In essence, all business relationships are based on trust. If you break the trust, the relationship goes away. People understand that mistakes happen. They can live with them, but they rarely stand by someone who breaks their trust. You build trust by telling customers what they can expect from you and fulfilling those expectations over and over again.

Communicate With Respect and Candor

In 1997, Oprah Winfrey asked Steven Spielberg how he could use such an unknown actor in a key role in his most recent film, *Amistad*. As you know, Spielberg is one of the cofounders of DreamWorks, a multi-billion dollar entertainment company. *Amistad* was one of the company's first films. Oprah Winfrey was really asking how in the world Spielberg could use such an unknown actor in such an unbelievably important role. Spielberg said the person was a very good actor and he really enjoyed working with him. He said that if he is going to spend six months making a film, he wants to enjoy being with the actors. Ultimately, he was talking about the value of a person's ability to communicate with respect and candor.

Faculty Input From "Corporate Catalysts University"

Mary Kay Ash, founder of Mary Kay Cosmetics, said, "Listening is an art. And the first tenet of the skill is that undivided attention to the other party. When someone enters my office to speak with me, I don't allow anything to distract my attention. You've got to pay attention in order to hear what the other person is saying. Without discipline and concentration, our minds wander" (*The Book of Business Wisdom* by Peter Krass, John Wiley & Sons, 1997).

Bill Marriott, Jr., wrote in his book, *The Spirit to Serve* (HarperBusiness, 1997), "After more than forty years in business, I've concluded that listening is the single most important on-the-job skill that a good manager can cultivate. A leader who doesn't listen well risks missing critical information, losing (or never winning) the confidence of staff and peers, and forfeiting the opportunity to be a proactive, hands-on manager."

Dick Vermeil, the head coach of the 2000 Super Bowl Champion St. Louis Rams, said, "To me, you measure the morale of an organization by the person making the least amount of money in the organization. If you're doing a real good job of communicating and making them realize that their contributions are important, then their morale will be good. The one thing I hope that I've been able to implant here is the core of the reason we're successful: the people, and caring about them and not being afraid to tell them that you care about them. To get teams to play to their full potential, I think it takes players who care about each other, mutual give-and-take, communication, and caring back and forth for the whole organization." (Source: *St. Louis Post-Dispatch*, January, 2001)

There's three pieces of advice from three different industries all making the same point: business is all about relationships.

14 Principles of Effective Communication

1. Share the conversation.

Maintain a natural balance between sharing your ideas and listening to the other person while she shares her ideas.

2. Talk the other person up.

Point out the really good things the other person has done. Do this especially behind his back, because you know it will get back to him.

3. Get to know them as human beings.

Find out what motivates, excites, challenges, and frustrates the other person.

4. Be excited about his or her dreams.

If the other person is going after a major dream, such as having a first child or building a new home or going on a dream vacation, get excited for her.

5. Value every role.

Every role in an organization is important. If you don't believe a particular role adds value, work to get rid of the role. As long as the role exists, value what the person in that role has to say.

6. Honor their differences.

Practically every business group has great diversity in terms of knowledge, experience, and talent. Respect those differences and be open to learning from every member of your group.

7. Respect their time and schedules.

People are not always available the minute you want to talk with them. One time I did a three-hour seminar for a group of 10 people, when all of a sudden, three of the participants were pulled out of the room for more than half an hour to find a memo that had been written six months earlier and had already been destroyed. Their supervisors did not respect their time and schedules.

8. Use clear, concise, and compelling messages.

Over the past seven years, I've interviewed more than 500 people at all levels in more than a dozen industries. One of the few common denominators is that everyone is very, very busy. No one has time to waste. Provide clear, concise, and compelling messages that are relevant and to the point. This is particularly true in voice mails, e-mails, and big speeches.

9. Appreciate ideas (accept suggestions as significant input).

Every idea has the potential to dramatically improve results in your highest-priority outcomes. Be open to ideas from everyone and don't worry about the other person's title.

10. Close the loop.

The most frequent complaint I hear about managers is that they don't close the loop. Many times, a manager asks an employee for his or her opinion, the employee goes out on a limb and becomes vulnerable by offering five ideas to the manager, and the manager never gets back to the employee with any kind of response. Closing the loop means the manager considers the input and gets back to the employee in a timely fashion with an answer as to which ideas will be enacted and why they were selected, and which ideas will not be enacted and why they were not selected.

11. Totally listen.

Totally listening is at the very heart of great communication. It means not thinking about what's going to happen next week while you're in the midst of a conversation. It means being fully present for the other person.

I've conducted a simple exercise in my seminars more than 300 times where I pair members of the audience together, have each person listen to the other for one minute, and have each person tell the other what they can remember. I then ask them what the experience was like to have someone really listen to them for one whole minute. One of the best answers I ever heard was from Linda Sue in South Bend, Indiana. She said, "To really listen, you almost have to be quiet for a minute." I asked her why she felt this way, and she replied, "In normal conversation, I talk for about eight seconds, then the other person talks for about eight seconds, and then I'm back talking again. However, there really is no time to listen because first I'm talking, and then while the other person is talking I have to think about what I'm going to say during my next eight seconds, and then I'm talking again. To really listen, you have to be quiet for at least a minute."

12. Clarify expectations (values, strategic alignment, results).

Without this clarity, the other person can work incredibly long and hard and yet never receive any praise for her efforts. You must clarify what you expect or you will continually create greater frustration.

13. Be honest.

A lack of honesty has cost corporations and shareholders billions of dollars. When you're always honest, people can trust you. If you lie or hold back the truth even once, people will always wonder if you're telling the truth.

14. Be genuinely enthusiastic.

You can't be truly great at something unless you're passionate about it. Let your passion and enthusiasm shine through so other people can see it.

10 Great Ways to Ruin Business Relationships

If you want some really great ways to ruin business relationships, here you go:

1. Dominate the conversation.

Do all of the talking and don't let the other person talk at all. It sends a very clear message you really don't care what the other person has to say.

2. Stay in your comfort zone.

If you have an idea that would make your organization or your customer more successful than they have ever been before, don't share it. Keep it to yourself.

3. See only the other person's faults.

Focus only on what is wrong with the other person.

4. Smash the conversation into the other person's face.

Yell things such as, "That's the way it's going to be so just deal with it," and "My mind is made up, and that's the end of the discussion." It might really be the end of the discussion, but it also might be the end of the relationship.

5. Simply don't pay attention.

Make good eye contact, smile, and nod your head, but when the other person gets done talking, have absolutely no idea what they just said.

6. Tear the other person down behind his or her back.

This is a particularly effective way to ruin a business relationship. Rip on someone over and over again, especially behind their back, because you know it's going to get back to them.

7. Use negative nonverbal communication.

While the other person is talking, roll your eyes, stare at the ceiling, and sigh a lot. It sends the message you cannot wait until they get done talking.

8. Maintain an attitude of arrogance.

This topic could fill an entire book. Arrogance conveys that you believe you already know everything there is to know about a topic. The old-fashioned way to be arrogant is to respond to every idea with, "We tried that idea years ago, and it will never work."

Technology provides an array of ways to be arrogant. For example, by leaving an e-mail with 10 different 10-page attachments, you basically say your input is so valuable other people should give up 90 minutes reading it. If you really want to be arrogant, leave a four-minute voice mail where you speak very, very slowly. However, leave your phone number in the middle of the voice mail and say it very, very fast so the other person has to listen to it over and over again.

9. Break your promises.

Another classic way to ruin relationships is to tell someone you will do something on a certain day and you don't do it. Or you tell the person you will call them and you never get back to them.

10. Make throwaway comments frequently.

As I mentioned earlier, managers can really put their foot in their mouth after their prepared statements. They feel good about their speech, relax, and then—boom—they say something they regret. Remember Jimmy Carter's infamous line about lusting after women in *Playboy* magazine? He said that as the interviewer walked out of his house.

Corporate Catalyst Tip #6:
Why Most Managers Lose Their Jobs

Of the last 10 managers I knew who got fired, all 10 lost their jobs because of poor communication skills. Their responsibilities ranged from running multi-billion dollar business units to managing a staff of five people, but the root cause of their failures ran along similar paths. Their communication issues ranged from intense abrasiveness to constantly being late to dominating every conversation to belittling their group members to eroding productivity through endlessly long meetings. A person with superb communication skills and average technical skills always accelerates past the person with superb technical skills and average communication skills.

The Realities of Teamwork

Teamwork is the rare corporate occurrence. Teamwork happens when the members of a group share a common objective and work together to support each other's efforts toward the achievement of that objective. Sounds so easy, and yet it rarely happens in a business setting. More often, members of the group focus on their own individual objectives and justify their actions in relation to these desired outcomes. Customers don't care about individual goals and activities. They only care about receiving value from their purchases.

One time I asked a flight attendant what it was like to work for Southwest Airlines. She said she loved it. I challenged her by asking, "You love it? Why do you love it?" She said, "I used to work for another airline, and when we had meetings, everyone sat by their department: flight attendants here, pilots there, and mechanics over there. At Southwest Airlines, we sit all over the place. Everybody knows what we're trying to achieve and everybody works together to make it happen." That's teamwork.

The purpose of building great teamwork within a corporation is to achieve better business results. Period. There is no other reason to invest the time, talent, energy, and financial resources necessary to achieve great teamwork. Consequences such as enhanced self-esteem or feeling better about the people you work with are nice, but they are not the purpose of building stronger teamwork within a business. The desired end result is better business outcomes.

From this perspective, building great teamwork is as important to a corporation's short-term and long-term success as enhancing a certain aspect of operations, implementing a successful marketing initiative, or reducing costs through eliminating waste.

Benefits of Outcome-Based Teamwork

➢ Develop breakthrough ideas.

A collaborative atmosphere is a characteristic of a great team. Not only does each player bring his or her best ideas forward, he or she also listens to the other ideas presented, and the team collectively generates even more powerful ones. This constant exchanging, refining, and combining of ideas leads to far more profitable ways of doing business. Rather than being captured in a department silo, ideas have the opportunity to travel across departments and be immediately improved before hitting the marketplace. One successful breakthrough idea can produce a dramatic impact on an organization's bottom line.

➢ Attract and retain top performers.

The need to attract and retain great talent represents one of the hardest organizational challenges. With so many options available, why would any superbly talented person stay in an organization where he or she feels stifled by politics, bureaucracy, and top-down management? Being part of a great team environment, making a positive difference, and having extraordinary opportunities to apply unique skills are reasons to stay at an organization. The long-term financial impact of attracting and retaining top performers is staggering. The cost of continually recruiting and training new employees combined with the loss in productivity and innovations due to losing top performers devastates a corporation's profit and loss statement.

➢ Strengthen long-term customer relationships.

You positively affect profits through retaining your best customers. There is a direct correlation between the companies who have high employee retention and those who have high customer retention. People like familiarity. Customers want to work with people they trust and know well. Customers enjoy working with people who are enthusiastic about what they do and where they work.

Characteristics of Great Business Teams

➢ **Individuals enjoy the environment.**

On a great team, employees are excited to work together. Fun doesn't happen when employees stand around the coffee pot complaining about other people. You create an enjoyable work environment when your employees work on meaningful projects, their ideas are listened to and respected, and there is an absence of backstabbing and whining. People enjoy exchanging their ideas on a concept when they feel they won't be reprimanded later for what they said. People have fun when they get to run with an idea that fits within the overall strategy. It is up to you to create and maintain this atmosphere.

➢ **Individuals feel they belong.**

When individuals feel they belong in a group, their willingness to commit their time, talent, and energy to the bigger cause goes up dramatically. If they feel like outsiders, they are less likely to do anything more than what is necessary. This sense of camaraderie can be enhanced through orientation, internal mentoring programs, participation on focus groups and committees, project assignments, role reversals, and social events. The key is for the individual to look at the other team members and feel they fit in and want to be with them.

> **Individuals feel they are significant.**

On great teams, each individual feels the team would somehow be worse off if he or she left the group. People leave organizations when they do not feel significant. They leave when they get the impression it really doesn't matter whether they stay or not. When a person feels significant, she believes she must give her best effort or the team will suffer. If the person feels insignificant, he justifies being late, calling in sick, or giving a poor performance because he doesn't think his efforts really matter anyway. You need to identify what specific value each team member brings to the group, and publicly and privately reward that value. You must also continually provide meaningful opportunities for each individual to step forward and provide greater value.

> **Individuals trust the other members of the group.**

The quickest possible way to ruin a great team is to break the trust people have with one another. You can easily accomplish this by breaking your promises or tearing another person down behind their back. Trust is the glue that maintains the cohesiveness of a great team. Without trust, talented individuals focus their attention inward, create silos with their departments, and dramatically reduce the creative energy they give toward accomplishing the team objectives. Building trust is the responsibility of every team member.

> **Individuals believe in the purpose of the group.**

When members strongly believe in the reason why their group exists, they stretch to give their very best effort. This goes beyond profit, salaries, and recognition. If a person connects with the group's purpose, their creative juices flow and they find ways to succeed. Without a clear sense of purpose, group members shift to tangential goals and the group's end result reflects this lack of a coordinated effort.

You need to periodically pull your team away from daily activities and have them identify why the team exists, what they want to accomplish, and why these desired achievements have value. By clarifying the team's purpose through open discussion, the commitment level of the members goes up. This does not have to be a definitive answer. The group may come back at a later date and alter the sense of purpose. The key is that they do it together.

> **Individuals feel being part of the team enhances their futures.**

This isn't communism. Top performers still want to achieve great results over the long term. They never want to feel stuck with a group. Therefore, they need to believe being part of this team increases their chances for greater success in the future. When they start to feel the team hurts their future opportunities, they look for ways to leave. Consequently, you need to clarify a connection between each team member's present activities and his or her future opportunities. These opportunities could be at your organization or other ones.

Faculty Input From "Corporate Catalysts University"

Mike Krzyzewski, head basketball coach at Duke University, is one of the most successful coaches in NCAA history. He believes coaching is far more psychological than tactical, far more about leading from the heart than explaining Xs and Os. In his book, *Five-Point Play: Duke's Journey to the 2001 National Championship* (with Donald Phillips, Warner Books, 2001), he wrote, "The real secret of this season's success was our five-point play—which we symbolized with a fist. There are five fundamental points that can help make a team great: communication, trust, collective responsibility, caring, and pride. I like to think of each as a separate finger of THE FIST. Any one individually is important. But all of them together are formidable."

The Ups and Downs of Disasters

Perhaps no event generates effective teamwork faster than dealing with a catastrophe. Without hesitating, people willingly take roles they otherwise would not consider and superbly fulfill their responsibilities. Members of the group feel a sense of purpose that they have never felt before. They listen to other people's ideas, regardless of their title, and share their ideas even if they seem a little crazy.

In 1993, a horrendous flood wreaked unbelievable damage on the St. Louis area. In response, people of all races and economic situations stood shoulder-to-shoulder and packed sandbags. During that horrible experience, people set aside their stereotypes and simply focused their collective efforts on the greater good. That's the upside of disasters: they bring people together like never before.

The downside of disasters is that the positive outcomes don't last. In the absence of a disaster, members of the group have to create a sense of purpose and work collaboratively to create true teamwork. This requires proactive effort versus the reactive work done in dealing with a disaster. The truly great teams do not need a disaster to instill collaborative efforts. Truly great teams sustain their level of teamwork far longer than teams formed through disasters, because disasters are not sustainable stimulants.

Convert Negative Conflict Into Productive Collaboration

The two primary reasons disagreements escalate into nasty conflicts are:

- Each individual becomes emotionally attached to his or her side of the argument.
- Each individual only sees the topic from his or her perspective.

In other words, each individual stays mired in his or her narrow, subjective, and emotional aspects of the issue. As long as both sides stay in that mindset, they either attack the other individuals or blindly defend their viewpoints. No real collaboration can ever occur in this manner. Leaders create true collaboration, an exchange of ideas that builds even better ideas, by getting each individual to move toward a broad, objective, and rational point of view.

Conflict to Collaboration Exercise

Here's an exercise to teach your employees the method for moving from conflict to collaboration that I described earlier:

First, break your overall group into small groups of three people, and have each group choose one of the following topics: sports, shopping, films, or the Internet. After they select their topic, have everyone in the small group work together to come up with a list of reasons why it is the worst thing for young people. Remind them to do this even if they don't agree it is the worst thing for young people. After a few minutes, ask everyone to work with their small group members to come up with a list of reasons why their topic is the best thing for young people. After a few more minutes, ask them to discuss what the experience was like for them.

At this point in the exercise, people usually say they see both sides of the argument from a broader perspective and are less emotionally attached to either one of them.

Immediately follow this non-business discussion with a real business situation for them to analyze. Have the large group clarify two perspectives on the issue. Then have the members of each small group come up with a list of reasons supporting each of the perspectives. Finally, ask everyone to discuss what can be done to optimize the situation toward generating better sustainable results.

Based on my experience in using this exercise, I believe your group will develop a better solution than they had before the meeting because they will see the situation from a broader, more objective, and more rational perspective.

Another way to generate greater collaboration is to have members of cross-functional teams spend a day or two in the other person's role. Have a marketing person spend two days attending operational meetings, visiting various sites, and stepping into the world of an operations manager. A week later, have the operations manager spend two days attending marketing meetings and watching how marketing ideas move from concept to implementation. Each person will probably develop a greater understanding of the other person's function and valuable insights for the other person to consider.

THE CORPORATE CATALYSTIC CONVERTER

☑ Every business is in the relationship business.

No industry exists where people don't interact with other people. Even if your contact with customers is completely done via the Internet, you still must build relationships with customers in order to drive sustainable and profitable growth.

☑ You build business relationships by learning about the other person, understanding what they need, clarifying what they can expect from you and your organization, and fulfilling those expectations.

☑ Effective communication includes respect, candor, listening for understanding, and always being honest.

☑ Many managers who get fired for performance issues have done a poor job of communicating.

The great communicator with average technical skills always outpaces the great technician with average communication skills. Of course, having both doesn't hurt, either.

☑ Members of groups create teamwork when every member supports every other member toward the achievement of a common goal.

This rare dynamic delivers great value to both the individuals and the organization. Maintaining teamwork requires constant focus on both the needs of the individuals and the overall group.

☑ Conflicts are not productive because they keep people stuck in the world of the narrow, emotional, and subjective.

Collaboration generates business-driving ideas that are broad, rational, and objective.

Recommended Resources for Corporate Catalysts

Leading with the Heart: Coach K's Successful Strategies for Basketball, Business, and Life by Mike Krzyzewski with Donald T. Phillips (Warner Books, 2000).

This is one of the very few books by an athletic coach I recommend to business people. Coach K successfully explains how concepts that work on the court also work in a corporation.

Russell Rules: 11 Lessons on Leadership from the Twentieth Century's Greatest Winner by Bill Russell with David Falkner (New American Library, 2002).

This is the other book from the world of sports that I recommend. Bill Russell's ideas are as applicable in the 21st century business environment as they were in the 1950s and 1960s basketball world. A great example is his idea of studying the game from the viewpoint of every position on the court.

The Spirit to Serve: Marriott's Way by J.W. Marriott, Jr. (Harper-Business, 1997).

Bill Marriott does a wonderful job explaining how all the different functions within a hotel need to support each other in delivering a great guest experience. This is a very down-to-earth explanation of teamwork in a massive corporation.

Chapter 7

HIRING IS NOT
THE DATING GAME

"IF WE GET THE RIGHT PEOPLE ON THE BUS, the right people in the right seats, and the wrong people off the bus, then we'll figure out how to take it someplace great."

This quote from Jim Collin's book, *Good to Great* (Harper-Business, 2001) has become one of the most popular sayings in modern corporations. I constantly hear executives talk about getting the right people on the bus and the wrong people off the bus. Every manager talks about the importance of people in driving better business results and yet far too many avoid putting in the time necessary to do it right. They turn this function over to the HR department and only focus on it when absolutely necessary.

If people truly are the most important assets in your organization, why wouldn't the attraction and retention of the right people be your number-one focus and the place where you dedicate most of your time? The reason I've witnessed goes back to the short-term mentality I wrote about in Chapter 1. Identifying the right people, developing them, and putting them in the right positions takes time and does not convert into better results in a week. Yet, if you do this week after week after week, you will develop an organization or department that generates incredible results. It comes down to getting a decent result today or an extraordinary result tomorrow. It's your call. The corporate catalysts always focus on generating significant, sustainable, and profitable growth. They understand some things need to be done today that won't pay off for a relatively long time.

The next thing managers usually say after quoting Jim Collins is, "So how do I do it? How do I know who these 'right people' are, and how do I know what positions to put them in?" To get the right people in the right seats on your bus, put your people-placement process through these three screens:

- ◆ Screen #1: Best Individuals.
- ◆ Screen #2: Best Mix.
- ◆ Screen #3: Best Positions.

Screen #1: Best Individuals

In order to get the "right" person in your organization or department, you need to decide what that person is like before you meet him or her. Otherwise, you may turn this process into *The Dating Game*—be seduced and end up married to a disaster for your work group.

The right person fits comfortably in *The Hiring Arena* shown in Figure 7.1.

The Hiring Arena

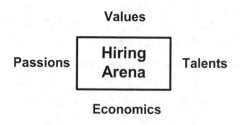

Figure 7.1

Parameters of The Hiring Arena:

1. Does the person have the values we want in our group or organization?

Remember, values are beliefs that determine behavior. Does this person have the beliefs and corresponding behaviors you want in your group?

2. Does this person have passion for the work he or she will be doing?

    Is he or she excited about this role, or just taking it for the paycheck?

3. Does this person have the talent to do the job he or she is being hired to do?

    The person doesn't need to have experience in this role, but he or she has to be able to do the job. Lou Gerstner had no background in the computer industry before he ran IBM, but he did a pretty darn good job.

4. Does the person's economic requirements match what the job has to offer?

    Does the person have to earn a certain amount today, or can he or she live with less today if it means a greater financial potential in the future? Compensation and benefits are important, and if this screen is not met properly in the short term, it could lead to a problem when you need the person the most.

The reason I put these questions in this order is because this is the order of importance in hiring the person. No matter how much talent and passion the person brings to the table, if they don't have the desired values, don't hire them. Values are like DNA, they rarely change. Initially, the new employee may seem like a great addition to your team, but applauding a person with the wrong behaviors generates a long-term and devastating ripple effect throughout your group and organization.

If the person does not have passion for the work, he or she probably will never develop it. It's possible, but very unlikely. It is far easier to develop the necessary skills for a role than passion for the job. Ask yourself three questions about the candidate:

+ Does he care about the work?
+ Does he understand the importance of the work in terms of what it adds to other people?
+ Is he dying to do the job?

The candidate will never achieve greatness in any role without passion, and she won't be promoted unless she does a great job.

If he has the values and passion, determine if he has the skill to do the job or the capacity to develop the skill. Incompetence will lead to frustration for the candidate, your group members, and yourself. While people generally either have the necessary values and passion or they never will have them, these same people can develop skills through training and experience. A lack of skill today may not be a good reason not to hire the person.

Finally, the economics need to be right on both ends. Overpaying for a person today can cause long-term problems in your organization in three ways:

+ If the person does a great job, he will expect a raise, even though you might feel he's already being paid to do a great job.

+ It can cause a great deal of resentment with other group members.

+ If you base bonuses on individual performances you can fall back into the EPS syndrome. I encourage you to base approximately half of bonuses on achieving outstanding results within a role and half on the group's performance.

The Process of Screening for the Right Individuals

You can use interview questions, role-playing, case studies, reference checks, and interaction with other employees to determine if a prospect is right for your organization. Take each of your organizational values and develop a few questions you could ask to gain an understanding of the other person. For each value, role-play a scenario with him and see how he behaves. Write up a theoretical business situation involving each of the values, have the other person read it, and ask him how he would handle it. Develop specific questions to ask his references to determine whether he has the values you want. Have the person interact with your employees and specifically look at how his behaviors relate to your group's desired values. Repeat this process of using questions, role-playing, case studies, reference checks, and interactions with group members to determine if he has the necessary passion and talent to succeed in this role.

Sample of the screening process for best individuals

Here's an example using "teamwork" as the desired value:

Interview Question: Ask, "How do the members of your work group achieve significant business goals in your current organization?"

Listen to find out whether the group achieved these results through a silo or team approach. You may need to follow up with more probing questions.

Role-Playing: Say, "You and I are working on developing a new product launch. I'm the head of marketing and you're the head of operations. What do you suggest needs to be done for us to be successful?"

As the role play unfolds, try to pull the person away from working in support of one another and see if they try to sell you on the value of working together. Then try pulling the person toward the value of teamwork and see if they try to downplay the importance of working together.

Case Study: Say, "Here's a scenario I'd like to get your feedback on. Two companies merged and combined employees under a single brand name who had been fierce competitors for more than 10 years. You have been named head of this new merged department with employees from both former companies. What will you do in the first 30 days?"

Listen for the values he emphasizes as he answers this question. It will tell you a great deal about how he will behave in the future.

Question for Reference: Ask her references, "How would you describe her approach to achieving high priority outcomes?"

In this manner, you don't tip your hand as to whether or not you want a team-oriented performer or a solo artist.

Interaction With Group Members: If possible, have the person attend one of your group's meetings on a relatively minor business issue. Don't give away your secrets, but see how he behaves in real group settings.

If you apply one or more of these five approaches for each of the desired values, passions, and talents, you will have a pretty good feel as to whether this person could succeed in your organization. Of course, all of this implies you already have done your homework in determining the type of values, passions, and talents you want in this position. If the person still fits within The Hiring Arena you've created for this position, begin to explore the economics of the situation. You may want to give her a preliminary understanding up front just so you don't waste each other's time. But the real nuts-and-bolts conversation about economics should wait until the end. By better understanding each other, you may both find you're willing to be flexible regarding compensation and benefits.

Every manager should do this process for the people they hire directly. If you're not in the HR function, don't put this hiring process on the human resources department to do in a silo. HR should play a role in assisting the process, but it should not be the driver for a key hire in your department. In addition, a similar approach should be applied to every current employee. Make sure you have the "right" people already on board. You might have employees who are relatively inexpensive and can do the technical work involved, but who don't have the desired values or passions necessary for long-term success. You may think you're winning, but, in reality, you may substantially hurt your sustainable, profitable growth by keeping the wrong people.

Screen #2: Best Mix

The key is to optimize diversity. Not just in terms of gender and race, but in a host of other areas as well. Notice I said "optimize diversity" and not "maximize diversity." Maximizing diversity means you have every type of person represented in your group. This can actually slow progress if it gets carried too far. Having an organization filled with clones of the boss can generate short-term success, but nullify long-term growth. Having a group filled with vast ranges of diverse thoughts and approaches can cause the operation to never move forward. Optimizing diversity means deciding on the desired mix that will drive your business forward and working to hire those people.

Diverse Aspects of Diversity

1. Gender.

Have a mix of male/female employees as close to 50/50 as you can. In my experience, the closer an organization gets to all-male or all-female, the less collaboration actually occurs.

2. Race.

Racial diversity is a business driver, not a strategy in political correctness. With the advance of the Internet, more and more companies do work throughout the United States and around the world. Racial diversity is one way to include a broader understanding of underlying and oftentimes invisible issues that affect an organization's interactions with customers.

3. Cultural.

Racial diversity created by hiring people who all live in the same area may not include viewpoints from different cultures. If your products or services are sold to multiple cultures, work to hire people who have experience in these cultures. For that matter, even if your organization doesn't sell to multiple cultures, try to broaden the perspective of your group by hiring people with different cultural backgrounds. The flair this diversity adds to your group might be the missing piece you've always needed.

4. Personality.

If your group is composed of all "quick decision-makers," your group may make quick decisions that lose a lot of money. Of course, if you have all "conscientious decision-makers," you may never get anything done. The ideal group has a mixture of all four types of decision-makers.

5. Strengths.

Some people effectively deal with conflict, while others excel at tackling details. Some people like to organize huge meetings and some people prefer communicating in private conversations. Look at the strengths of the members of your group, look at the strengths of the person you're considering hiring, and ask yourself if this person will add anything special to make your group better.

6. Experiences.

Do some members of your group have experience working inside huge corporations, while others have experience running start-up entrepreneurial ventures? Have some people been on record-setting sales teams, while others have dealt with sales disasters? If you have 50 employees and they all have the same experience, you really have the same experience 50 times. When people have very different experiences, they can add real insights to move the business forward.

Screen #3: Best Positions

When I was a college and high school soccer coach, the other coaches and I spent an inordinate amount of time writing on napkins. We would draw up the starting lineup one way and then start making changes. By switching players around and inserting other names into the lineup, we saw the potential of our team from a variety of perspectives. Sometimes we would put our fastest players at forward and our tallest players in the back. Sometimes we would put our most skillful players on the outside positions and our physically strongest players on the inside. We would mix our lineup over and over again by trying different combinations in practice and even in some of the games. Our rationale was pretty simple. We never wanted an injury to a key player to keep us from having other people prepared to play that position. We also wanted to find out as much as we could about each player. Many times, a star forward at one age level turned out to be mediocre at the next level. However, having been a forward helped him to be an even better defender for us.

Hiring the right people both on an individual basis and in terms of what makes the best makeup for your team is not enough. In order to optimize the success of your organization, keep exploring for the best possible positions for each person. You also need to be ready for the "run over by a bus" scenario. In other words, if something happened to one of your employees, would you have someone else ready to step in? Another benefit of experimenting with people in different positions is that they develop a broader understanding of the organization and can add better insights.

Ways to Clarify the Best Positions

Role requirement approach

Here's a four-step filtering process to get people in the right positions:

1. Identify the highest priority business outcome.
2. Identify the responsibilities each role needs to fulfill in order to improve this outcome.
3. Make a list of the people who could fulfill these responsibilities either right now or with some training.
4. Try new people in that position. If only one person does it forever, you have no backup plan, no diverse perspectives, and no experienced person to replace a potentially burnt-out person currently in the role. Force yourself to move a qualified operations person who wants to try a role in marketing into the marketing function. This may be very difficult in the short term, but could reap great dividends in the long term.

Short-term trial

Get in the habit of rotating people throughout the organization for a day or two each quarter. For example, have the HR person spend a few days shoulder-to-shoulder with an operations person. Let them sit in operational meetings, see what problems pop up on the operations radar screen, and observe how they get resolved. Then have the person join the marketing team and the research team and so on. Do the same with people from other departments. The more people can experience their business life from other people's perspectives, the better they understand the business. They start to see what other parts of the business might interest them, and they may also see the business in a way that allows them to offer better suggestions.

Case Study: A Classic Case of Successful Succession-Planning

At the 2004 worldwide conference of McDonald's owner/operators and employees, Jim Cantalupo, CEO of McDonald's, was scheduled to make opening remarks at 9:30 a.m. He passed away of a heart attack at 3:30 a.m. Within six hours of his death, the McDonald's board of directors appointed Charlie Bell the new CEO. Charlie Bell had been the COO of the company. The succession plan was clearly in place. This was one of the ultimate examples of why depth charts are critically important. It doesn't really matter if you're talking about the CEO of a major corporation or an hourly employee who calls in sick. If you don't have a depth chart in hand, you'll search for a replacement while your customers wait. Of course, customers only wait for so long before they move on.

Corporate Catalyst Tip #7:
Always Have a Depth Chart

Your success as a manager greatly depends on the quality of the people in your group. The key question is, "How do you constantly increase the quality of the people in your group?" Keep in mind, at any time, you could lose a good employee to another organization or another part of your organization. One key to success is to always have a depth chart in hand.

Make a list of all the positions in your group. For each position, have a list of at least three people who can do the job well. These could be people in your group, in your organization, or even outside of your organization. The first name for each position is the person currently in that spot. Put at least two more names of people who fall inside The Hiring Arena for that position. You can have some names on the depth chart in more than one position. Of course, if you have the same name as the number-one backup for every position, you really don't have much depth. By doing this, you quickly see whether you need to develop some of your employees for other possible roles. It also forces you to see the importance of constantly looking for passionate, talented people outside your organization. Every manager should identify potential employees as much as they do potential customers.

THE CORPORATE CATALYSTIC CONVERTER

☑ The "right" person for one organization is definitely the "wrong" person for another organization.

You have to determine what the "right" person is like for your group or organization. The four critical factors in determining the "right" person are values, passions, talents, and economic desires. The four key questions to determine whether or not a person is right for your group are:

- Will they behave in a way that will make us proud to have them on our team?
- Do they want to do the job?
- Can they do the job?
- Can we meet their financial short-term and/or long-term goals?

☑ In order to optimize the effectiveness of your group or organization, optimize diversity.

Optimal diversity creates a chemistry that generates continually better ideas, behaviors, and results. As you hire people, make sure they enhance the mixture within the group.

☑ The ultimate team has depth at every position and people who understand each other's roles.

This can only happen by moving people around and having them experience aspects of the business from multiple positions, even if only for a few days. Their enhanced skills and perspectives can help drive the business to new heights.

☑ Apply just as much rigor in determining whether your current employees are the right people in the right positions as you do with your hiring decisions.

☑ Allocate a significant portion of your time to search for new talent and develop the skills of your current employees.

Recommended Resources for Corporate Catalysts

Jack: Straight From the Gut by Jack Welch with John Byrne (Warner Business Books, 2001).

This is an extraordinary book about how to run a massive corporation. At times it seems overly simplistic, it borders on the unbelievable and I disagree with the 20/70/10 Rule, but Jack Welch definitely provides an amazing case study on how to assess people, get them in the right positions and develop a depth chart. I encourage you to read it, study it, and think about how some of the central themes apply to the people in your organization.

The
Challenge

Chapter 8

"CHANGE IS GOOD" AND OTHER CORPORATE NONSENSE

THE PURPOSE OF THIS CHAPTER is to identify and eliminate corporate nonsense. Corporate catalysts clearly understand that accelerating critical business outcomes involves not doing some things as much as doing other things. By understanding and avoiding corporate nonsense, corporate catalysts can focus more of their time, energy, and resources on doing the few things that really drive sustained improvement in key results.

25 Examples of Corporate Nonsense

Corporate Nonsense #1: Change Is Good

Yeah, right. Tell that to the single parent with two kids in high school who just found out she can only keep her job if she's willing to move 500 miles to a new location. Tell that to the 50-year-old computer programmer who just lost his job to a person half his age from overseas who will work for 70 percent less money. Tell that to the television industry as commercials lose their relevance due to digital video recorders.

Change is NOT always good. Repeat after me. Change is NOT always good. Change, even small changes, can wreak extraordinary havoc in people's lives. Trying to pretend it's always good causes you to live in a fairyland where reality becomes skewed and you avoid dealing with harsh reality. The longer you postpone dealing with changes, the harder it becomes to mount any sort of momentum. Telling people that change is good for everyone causes you to lose credibility in their eyes.

Corporate Correction:
Change is inevitable, so get used to it

Get down to reality as quickly as possible. Sometimes change is very hard, but it is inevitable. Consequently, create changes in your life on a regular basis and better prepare yourself for when the unforeseen change occurs. Ask yourself, "What is something I could change in my life right now?" Make the change and begin to deal with the repercussions. Perhaps it means pursuing a lower-paying job in your organization that will broaden your understanding of the business and the industry. Perhaps it means trying a new hobby. Do something to regularly create change in your life. The skills you develop in dealing effectively with change can be very valuable when change is thrust on you.

Corporate Nonsense #2: Customers Are Always Right

No, they're not. A customer ranting and raving in your face is not always right. Bending over backward and lowering your self-esteem to deal with an angry customer does not benefit anyone. If you lower your price just because customers demand it, you actually hurt your long-term relationship with them because now they're wondering if you lied to them in the first place. If you create a whole new package of value to get them to calm down, you have solved the short-term issue and created a massive long-term problem as every other customer will want the same deal.

Corporate Correction:
Customers provide valuable perspective

Every complaint provides another clue into outside perspective. Each one is valuable and needs to be considered. However, you don't have to give in to every complaint. In resolving a complaint, protect your self-esteem, try to diffuse the customer's emotions, and deal with the problem efficiently and effectively. This may mean refunding the customer, or it may mean letting the customer know you can't do anything and why you can't. A customer relationship is like a personal relationship. If you always apologize and give in to even the most ridiculous complaint, the other person will lose respect for you. Gain the customer's perspective, consider it, and then do what you think is appropriate.

Corporate Nonsense #3: CEOs Must Be Superheroes

This myth caught fire in the early 1980s during Lee Iaccoca's reign at Chrysler, and grew to ridiculous proportions in the late 1990s. Even after the CEO disasters at HealthSouth, WorldCom, Enron, Tyco, Adelphia, Parmalat, and so on, CEOs still get paid exponential versions of king's ransoms. Why? It goes back to the quick fix, silver bullet mentality that fixates far too many organizations. People think they need someone to come into their organization and make them great. They feel they need a savior, a turnaround expert, and they're willing to pay anything to get the right person. Then, if things don't go well, they just fire that person. Even at lower levels in an organization, the same mentality presides. Far too often, people feel if the right person is put in charge, everything will go great. Rather than examining the other potential systemic issues involved, they just fire the old boss, turn things over to the new boss, and hope for a turnaround.

Corporate Correction: CEOs need to be effective

A CEO is an executive. An executive is a person who makes decisions. Organizations need effective executives. Therefore, they need executives to make decisions that improve the significant, sustainable, and profitable growth of their organizations. They don't need playboys, rock stars, massive egos, or liars at the top. Because of their status, some CEOs get away with incredibly stupid things for incredibly long periods of time. No one wants to tell them they're acting like asses. The same thing happens at every level. If you're in charge of a group, make effective decisions instead of making a complete fool of yourself.

Corporate Nonsense #4: One Plus One Equals Three

We hear the same mantra at the beginning of every merger. Someone says, "One plus one will equal three in the new organization. By combining resources, we will cut staff, cut overhead, cut expenses, and drive profitability." Sounds like the unbridled optimism of NFL teams on draft day. Unfortunately, mergers work out at about the same rate as first-round draft choices. In other words, their success rate is not very predictable. Merging two corporations does not guarantee success. It's a risky proposition filled with lots of potential downside.

Corporate Correction:
One plus one can equal zero, so be careful

Mergers are effective if people from the two separate cultures can define the value the new group will contribute to customers and determine how they will support one another in delivering that value. If you're not careful, the new group will lose an enormous amount of time fighting over which way to do tasks. If you merge organizations or departments, be sure to clarify the New Playing Field from the very beginning. Clarify the expected values, strategy, short-term objectives, and long-term objectives. Don't assume people from two different former teams will just "work things out" on their own. Coach key individuals as the new group moves forward. Hold people accountable for operating within this new playing field. Never assume the merged organization or group will move forward flawlessly.

Corporate Nonsense #5: Time Management Drives Better Results in Your HPOs

Managing your time is not a panacea for improving your highest priority business outcomes. You can have a clear checklist of what needs to be done today and tomorrow and next week, you can execute everything on your checklist flawlessly, and you can still get terrible results. Good time management does improve efficiency, but it doesn't necessarily improve effectiveness.

Corporate Correction:
Priority management increases effectiveness

Organizing your time is important, but you will only improve critical results by managing your priorities. Keep in mind *The 1-3-6 Rule*, which asks these three questions:

1. What is the highest priority business outcome you want to improve?
2. What three things can you do that would have the greatest positive impact on achieving that outcome?
3. What six things do you need to stop doing so you have the time, energy, and resources to do the three things you know you need to do in order to improve the desired results?

Once you know your answers to these three questions, manage your time so you do the three things that matter and avoid the six things that don't matter.

Corporate Nonsense #6: Go the Extra Mile

How many times have you heard, "If at first you don't succeed, try, try again"? According to this fallacy, *you* are the reason you're not getting the desired result, and all you have to do is keep trying in order to achieve it. That's goofy. Maybe there are a hundred other reasons why you haven't achieved the desired result. While there is something to be said for putting your nose to the grindstone, it can also be a terrible way to lose perspective on the big picture. The employee who works and works and works at a problem without ever stepping back is not a corporate catalyst.

Corporate Correction: If at first you don't succeed,
try again, and then try something else

I like the old quote that says, "The first sign of insanity is doing the same thing over and over again and expecting different results." Use your desired outcome to help determine if you're acting effectively. If the outcome is not improving no matter how many times you repeat the experiment, try something else. I'm not suggesting you give up. I am suggesting you try a different path.

Case Study: How This Book Came to Life

In December 1990, I announced to my classmates at the Dale Carnegie course on effective public speaking that I was going to write a book. I told them I would write it within two years. Two years passed by and no book. Three more years went by and I self-published a booklet, but not a commercially published book. Six more years passed by and I kept talking about writing a book. In year 11, I wrote a book proposal, contacted literary agents, and was rejected over and over and over. Finally, one agent told me my book proposal had fallen behind his desk and he had just found it a year later. He said he wanted to represent me. I hurriedly sent him my updated book proposal. One year and many, many rejections later, we agreed to give up on that project. So I mailed him my third attempt. Seven months later, I received my first contract for a book, which that agent landed for me. The dream, which you're reading, had finally come true.

Notice that for *11* years I stuck blindly to the fallacy of, "If I just keep working at it and talking about it, it will eventually work out." During the next three years I tried a lot of approaches, and when one didn't work out, I moved on to something else. Sometimes you just have to stop banging your head against the wall and move to a different wall. I wish I had done so much earlier.

Corporate Nonsense #7: The Boss Is Always Right

Some people think they should never disagree with their bosses. I think this mindset traces back to the Great Depression, where just having a job seemed like a miracle, and employees never questioned their bosses for fear of losing their jobs. During the post–September 11th era, this mindset reemerged. Unfortunately, there are a lot of problems with never challenging your boss. You'll be perceived purely as a doer and not as a thinker. You'll be seen as the person to get a task done, but you'll never be considered for a promotion to upper management.

Corporate Correction: The boss might not want to be pushed back, but the goal is better results

The last time I checked, bosses are humans. Humans make mistakes; therefore, bosses make mistakes. Your boss got his or her position because of past performance. That past performance does not generate flawless thinking in all situations. If you truly think your boss's decision is wrong or less than optimal, offer your opinion. The very worst thing that can happen is your boss disagrees with you and overrides your input. Well, you could get fired, but that's not the worst thing, because why would you want to work for someone who won't consider alternatives? However, your boss might consider your input, make some adjustments, and generate better results for the organization. Who knows, you might even get some of the credit.

Corporate Nonsense #8:
Turn People Problems Over to HR

The human resources department has become the giant hole where all employee-related problems fall. Similarly, when revenues are down, executives turn the finger of blame at the sales and marketing people. When problems occur in the customer's experience, people expect the operations department to pick up the slack. This leads directly to the "silo" mentality that robs organizations of productive and profitable growth. Organizations generate sales by understanding the customer, clarifying to the customer what value they can expect in return for their investment, and delivering that value. The sales process requires integration between the sales, marketing, operations, and human resources departments. To slice the problems up and assign them to departments is like placing all the blame for the *Titanic* on the weather forecaster.

Corporate Correction: People problems disintegrate organizations and must be resolved organizationally

If you have problems with members of your sales team, analyze what that really means. Does it mean the salesperson has not taken the time to truly understand what the operations department can deliver? Does it mean the salesperson looks for the fast buck at the expense of the long-term customer relationship? Does it mean the salesperson doesn't really understand what is expected of her or she doesn't know how to do what is required of her? Was the mistake made during the hiring process or does the sales manager not hold the employee accountable?

People issues need to be analyzed first within a department, then between departments, and then by an "objective" third party, such as an executive overseeing the departments. A human resources employee can serve as a valuable adviser and facilitator through the process, but should not step in and make decisions about people in other departments.

Corporate Nonsense #9:
Go Where the Puck Is Going to Be

At the peak of his NHL career, Wayne Gretzky said, "I skate to where the puck is going to be, not where it has been." In other words, he anticipated where the next play was going to happen and got there before anyone else. As so often happens, executives tried to take this sports example and squeeze it into their business models. They quoted Gretzky any time they went after some fad in the marketplace. They rationalized not pursuing further expansion and improvement in their current line of business by saying they were simply going where the business will be in the future.

Unfortunately, this led companies on wild-goose chases all over the world. Dot-com companies, daily stock trades on the Internet, and reality television are just some of the examples where people got caught up in "the next great thing" and chased "opportunities" that had nothing to do with their core business or primary strengths.

Corporate Correction: Understand trends and how they affect your business

If you sell shoes, you want to understand the term "metrosexual" and how the fashion trends affect your business. However, if you sell baked goods, you don't want to try to force a trend into your business by making "metrosexual cupcakes." It sounds silly, but it's this kind of forced rationale that afflicts far too many businesses. Don't try to go where the trends are going unless they intersect with the value your business offers. If the trends affect your business, you can accelerate your achievements by altering your approach to the marketplace.

Corporate Nonsense #10: Maximize Every Opportunity

Many times, the mantra of "maximize every opportunity to grow your business" is thrown around like the Golden Rule. Unfortunately, maximizing an opportunity can put you out of business. For example, if a manufacturer creates a hot product and rushes to build new plants to support even greater manufacturing of that product, they may very well generate massive excesses of inventory that end up as waste. That waste can't be converted to anything productive and the manufacturer has to deal with an enormous debt. This used to happen in the housing industry on a regular basis when builders created huge inventories of houses and then got caught holding the bag when the market slowed. Today, most builders create a few spec homes and only build a new home after the sale has been made.

Corporate Correction: Optimize every opportunity

In other words, keep the picture of your overall business in mind. If you can convert an opportunity that fits within your core business into greater sales, do it, as long as it doesn't overwhelm your business. If this "hot" opportunity suddenly becomes your whole business, you are potentially in for a world of hurt. If the opportunity does not fit within the definition of your business, you are merely chasing fool's gold. Do you remember the story about the 1890s gold rush, where people gave up their careers to dig for gold only to find out that there were few winners and lots of losers? This happens when people overextend themselves to maximize an opportunity that doesn't fit their business model. For example, Global Crossing, a communications solutions company, maximized fiber-optic cable right into bankruptcy.

Corporate Nonsense #11: If You Build It, They Will Come

This was a great line in the film *Field of Dreams*, and it inspired millions of people to pursue their dreams. Unfortunately, it makes for a lousy business strategy. During the heyday of the dot-com era, people built thousands of office spaces to meet the frenzy of business travelers. Much of that additional space was wasted after September 11th, 2001. Simply building something extraordinary does not guarantee success. It can actually overextend a business and set it up for long-term failure. Management ego fuels many of these extraordinary creations more than customers' needs or wants.

Corporate Correction: If you create value, customers *might* come

A more realistic approach to business is to continually generate more value for customers and see if they respond to it. Keep in mind, there are no guarantees for success. Build new things, offer them to customers, and be willing to scrap the idea or make adjustments as needed. *Field of Dreams* had a happy ending because not only did Ray Kinsella's father show up, but so did thousands of paying customers. If the field hadn't resonated with customers, it would have been foolhardy to keep it forever. The same holds true for your pet projects. Be realistic and customer-centered, not ego-centered.

Corporate Nonsense #12: The Goal Is to Get Bigger

Corporations of all sizes obsess with getting bigger. For some reason, it just seems sexier to reel off bigger revenue numbers, number of employees, number of cities, number of clients, and so on. However, this obsession with growth can interfere with adding more value to customers, growing at a profitable pace, or securing a brighter long-term future. Remember that profitability is not about bringing in more money; it's about making more money. If it costs you two dollars to bring in an extra dollar in revenue, you have a quick-fix solution to bankruptcy.

Corporate Correction: The goal is to get better

Adding more clients and employees doesn't guarantee long-term profitable growth under the best of circumstances and can accelerate corporate collapse in the worst of scenarios. As you add new clients and new employees, make sure they fit within the framework of the purpose of your business. For example, if your business is built on speed of service, a person with an MBA from Harvard who moves very deliberately may not fit in very well. You're far better off improving within the defined purpose of your business than in just creating more short-term revenue.

Corporate Nonsense #13: Diversification Helps Reduce Risk

The theory goes that you shouldn't put all of your eggs in one basket. Instead, you should diversify your baskets so that if one falls apart, you still have others to fall back on. That makes good sense in putting together a financial portfolio, but not such good sense in running a business. This mindset leads corporations into all kinds of activities that have nothing to do with the purpose of their business. In recent years, both GE and Tyco have slowed down their diversification efforts and focused on growing revenues organically.

Corporate Correction: Diversifying your offerings under a common umbrella enhances your brand

Wal-Mart started out as a low-cost provider of consumer goods. Operating within that clear purpose, it has since moved into clothing, food, electronics, and so on. Today, they're the world's largest seller of chicken and DVDs. Wal-Mart continually diversifies the value it adds, but it does it under the umbrella of a common business purpose. MTV started out featuring just music videos, but has since expanded to interviews, award shows, and celebrity showcases. It also diversified its business under a single umbrella.

Corporate Nonsense #14: No News Is Good News

It used to be that not hearing from your boss or customers was a good thing. It meant you must not be doing anything wrong, and so your job was safe. With the number of communication outlets available today, if you don't hear from your boss or customers, you may very well be letting your important relationships slip away.

Corporate Correction: Difficult conversations imply trusting relationships

If you regularly have honest exchanges with your boss and customers, you know the relationship still exists. Think about your personal life. If you never hear from someone, you probably don't have much of a relationship with him or her. I can identify my best friends quickly because they are the ones who broach the difficult topics with me. In a professional and dignified manner, be honest with your clients and your boss. If they can't handle that, you don't have much of a relationship, and relationships are the foundation of significant, sustainable, and profitable growth. It means you need to work harder on strengthening these relationships or move on to a different situation.

Corporate Nonsense #15: The "20-70-10 Rule"

There are very few things I disagree with Jack Welch, former CEO of GE, on, but his "20-70-10 Rule" is definitely one of them. According to this rule, every manager within GE has to identify within his or her group the top 20 percent of the employees, the middle 70 percent, and the bottom 10 percent. Here's the real kicker: if you're in the bottom 10 percent of your group two years in a row, you have to leave the company. His rationale is this is done in the best interests of these bottom performers because they would never be able to move up within the group anyway, and, this way, they can get on with their careers. Huh? Seems to me if you have to get rid of your bottom 10 percent every year, you might as well fire the managers, because they're doing a lousy job of selecting and developing people. GE has the Darwinian Theory of Business. What if a manager actually does a great job of hiring and developing their employees and ends with all "A" players? Would he or she be better off hiring some "C" players every year, just to keep the lower brackets primed for future firings? GE dropped its once famous strategy that every one of its businesses had to be number one or number two in their industry, and I predict it'll drop this one as well.

Corporate Correction: Optimize every role

Managers have six jobs related to people: hire, develop, punish, reward, promote, and fire. Of course, a promotion is really a big reward and getting fired is really a big punishment. These responsibilities should never be stuffed into the rigidity of a formula. The manager should be held accountable for the quality of her team's performance, but should never be forced to fire a certain number of people each year. Sometimes a weaker performer provides a crucially important element to the group that it otherwise would not have in its makeup.

Corporate Catalyst Tip #8:
Challenge the Underlying Premise

Many times, people accept an outrageous business belief because no one challenges the underlying premise upon which it is based. When you hear someone say things have to be done a certain way, ask, "What is the premise you're basing that decision on?" Just by asking this question, you may cause the other person to rethink her position. If they have a weak underlying premise and still stick to the statement, point out the premise is just her opinion, and not a fact.

Corporate Nonsense #16:
Increased Responsibility Is a Good Thing

Your career is a microcosm of an organization. Just as an organization needs to have a clearly defined purpose in order to build its brand and long-term success, you need a purpose for your career. By simply taking on more responsibilities, you may become the jack-of-all-trades and master of none.

Corporate Correction: Intelligently adding and subtracting responsibilities can accelerate your career

Put additional responsibilities through the following filters:

* Will I be able to maintain the quality of my performance if I add these new responsibilities to my current ones?
* Do these new responsibilities fit within the framework of my values, passions, talents, and economics?
* Will doing these new responsibilities increase my chances to create the type of career I want to have over the long term?

If you get three yes answers, go for it. If not, think long and hard before you take on more responsibilities.

Corporate Nonsense #17:
Good Performers Make Good Managers

This might be the number-one reason why managers fail to succeed. For some reason, lots of executives assume a star salesperson or a star operations person will make a great manager. However, selling, executing operations, and managing a business unit require three distinct skill sets. Just as star baseball players rarely become great managers, there is no guarantee great functional performers will evolve into great business managers.

Corporate Correction: People with great management skills might become great managers

In Chapter 4, I wrote about the four responsibilities of a manager: define the Playing Field, coach, hold people accountable, and stay off of the field. To determine whether or not an individual should be promoted to a management position, examine her behaviors relative to these four responsibilities. Use these questions as a guide in assessing potential managers:

- Can she communicate clearly?
- Can she listen effectively and offer suggestions?
- Can she do the painful work of holding herself and other people accountable?
- Can she think strategically?
- Do her behaviors positively represent the corporate values?
- Can she get things done?
- Can she organize others to get things done?
- Can she stay out of the limelight and let others shine?

It's hard to turn down the star performer for a management role, but if she's not the best person for the position, you're making a mistake to promote her.

Corporate Nonsense #18: Never Say No to Your Boss

This is actually a corollary of earlier bits of nonsense. Far too often I hear employees complain they work too many hours. When I ask them why they do, they tell me it's because their boss makes them do it. Every time I hear this, I challenge their thought process. I explain that their boss wants better results, and if they keep doing far too many activities, they will never be able to do any of them very well. Consequently, their boss will get worse results, which will hurt their careers.

Corporate Correction: Clarify the HPOs with your boss

Sit down with your boss and get clarification on the highest priority business outcomes he or she wants improved. Give your input, challenge away, but at the end of the conversation, walk away supporting his or her final HPOs. Then when your boss wants you to do six more activities, explain which ones you will and won't be able to do and how your rationale connects back to the achievement of his or her HPOs. In other words, agree on the highest priority outcomes, but maintain autonomy over your schedule. You could get fired for refusing to do something, but the purpose of this book is to develop corporate catalysts, not organizational milquetoasts.

Corporate Nonsense #19: Take Care of Your People and They Will Take Care of Your Customers

It's not quite that simple. Treating your employees well does not automatically convert into them treating your customers well. Employees still have minds of their own and can act in any fashion they choose. It doesn't do any good for you to say, "I can't believe how these spoiled brats treat our customers after all I've done for them."

Corporate Correction: Hire, coach, and develop tour employees to take good care of your customers

By any measure, working at Disney World is hard work. Employees there are part of the show: they're cast members. They have to do their jobs with smiles and a passion for entertainment at all times on a daily basis. They consistently deliver value at an extraordinarily high level. How does the Walt Disney Company accomplish this? From the interview process through the orientation process through the ongoing evaluation process, cast members at Disney World are managed to deliver an extraordinary guest experience. A similar process generates extraordinary customer service at Marriott hotels around the world. It's not enough for managers to treat their people well. It's just as important they manage their employees to treat their customers well.

Corporate Nonsense #20: The More Successful a Corporation Becomes, the More Complex It Becomes

Usually, the more complex an organization becomes, the less successful it becomes. Compare Southwest Airlines to any of the other major airlines. Relatively speaking, Southwest Airlines has an extraordinarily simple approach to business: make travel fun, cheap, and convenient. Starbucks is a pretty simple concept to understand. So is Warren Buffett's approach to investing.

Corporate Correction: Simplicity drives sustainable growth

The most successful companies in the world identify what they can be extraordinary at, what would add value to their customers, and what drives their profitable growth. They look for the overlap of these three areas and operate within that area of focus. They drive even greater growth by innovating within this tight region and not allowing themselves to go off on tangents.

Corporate Nonsense #21: Increased Innovation Is a Business Outcome

In an interview in the April 19, 2004, issue of *BusinessWeek*, Bill Gates, chairman of Microsoft, said, "With our $6 billion a year (in research and development), we're doing more new things than anyone else. If growth is your story, you're looking in the wrong place. Now, if you're looking for innovation...we're more of a change agent for the way business is done, the way people work, the way people do things at home."

Unfortunately, all of this focus on innovation has simply led to more innovation, not to sustainable and profitable growth. For all of their billions of dollars invested in innovation, new business products and services were expected to generate less than $1 billion a year in 2004. In other words, innovating for the sake of innovating does not drive business results.

Corporate Correction: Innovation is a necessary tool toward driving improved HPOs

Innovation, the ability to continually create greater value for customers, is a crucially important element toward achieving significant, sustainable, and profitable growth. However, and this is a very big however, innovation is not an outcome. Working on your backhand may make you a better tennis player, but that's not an outcome. The outcome is winning more tennis matches. Don't lose sight of the forest, better business outcomes, by focusing on the trees, generating more innovation. The latter is important, but the former is what pays the bills. The more creative your employees are, the greater the chance they will view innovation as a high priority outcome. It's important for you to help them understand innovation is an important tool for driving business outcomes, but it is not an outcome in and of itself.

Corporate Nonsense #22: It Takes 21 Days to Develop a Habit

I wonder if anyone has ever scientifically tested this worn-out aphorism. It certainly doesn't support the reality I've seen. Many times, executives and managers tell me they want to do a better job of empowering their employees. They say they want to use more of a question-and-answer approach to get their employees to think for themselves. However, by the third month in a given quarter, they revert back to old habits and start telling their direct reports what to do and how to do it.

Corporate Correction: It takes two years to change behaviors for good

I've mastered the three-month diet program. Do you know this one? I eat very well six days a week for about three months. I exercise and start to pontificate about the value of a healthy lifestyle. I reach my weight goal, and then I start to lighten up on my self-discipline. About nine months later, I painfully reenter the three-month diet program. In other words, I've never developed my desired behaviors in this area.

In observing executives who want to change their behaviors, I've noticed they frequently go through a similar pattern. After about three months of using effective new behaviors, they take their habits for granted, start to slip a little here and a little there, and within about eight months, they're completely back to their old ways. I encourage you to stay the course for two solid years, and then you can rest reasonably assured you will stay on the new track for the long term.

Corporate Nonsense #23:
We Can Do More Than Other People

Over and over again, I hear executives say, "We can do more than other companies because we have better people." Invariably, that thought causes people to schedule more items on their meeting agenda, take on more new projects, and approach more issues than any five companies could reasonably handle.

For example, isn't it common sense that 15 people cannot reasonably discuss 18 agenda items in three hours? Yet this is exactly what happens in many meetings. When I suggest to managers they're trying to do too much during a meeting, they sometimes reply, "Yes, but we have to cover all of this material." Well, shoot, why don't they just add another 50 items? They'll cover those just about as well as the first 18.

Corporate Correction: Do less, achieve more

Rather than trying to break the Guinness Book of Records for number of agenda items checked off, focus on, at most, three important items every two hours. Provide people with information about these three items before the meeting, give them a few questions to think about before the meeting, and have open discussions during the meeting that leads to decisions being made and actions being executed.

Corporate Nonsense #24:
When You Have a Problem, Hire a Consultant

No, don't do that. Hiring a consultant to solve an important problem simply provides a short-term fix for to a long-term issue. For example, I no longer work with employees where the boss says, "Dan, we have a real problem with this person. Can you coach him or her?" I turn down the work and explain to the person that the real issue is a systemic one. Somewhere a breakdown occurred in the sequence of hiring, developing, and holding people accountable. If they want me to help them solve that systemic issue, I'm open to discussing it.

Corporate Correction: Hold consultants responsible for results, not methodology

If you invest in a consultant, you better expect an improved business result, and not just another new methodology. Before you hire a consultant, know what outcome you want the consultant to help you achieve. Know the value of the desired outcome in order to determine the expected return on investment in hiring the consultant. This helps you determine the parameters of the investment you're willing to make. Be doubly aware of consultants who want you to invest an enormous amount of your time and energy into doing things their way. A consultant should never merely solve a short-term problem. That's the job of a technician. A consultant should positively impact your long-term, sustainable, and profitable growth, or she shouldn't be there.

Corporate Nonsense #25: "If Only..., Then We'd Be a Success."

This is the ultimate corporate nonsense. When I speak at an organization's annual conference, I usually interview 12 to 15 members of the group before I speak. I ask, "In your opinion, what's going well here in terms of generating the desired business results, what's not going well, and what would make things better?"

I can quickly gain a pretty strong understanding of whether this is a great, mediocre, or poor company. The people at great companies point out how each department supports the others in driving better results. They talk about how people from different departments exchange ideas informally on a regular basis. They explain how things get done quickly and in the right way the first time.

At poor companies, everyone plays the "If only..." game. These people say, "If only the president would communicate better, then we'd be a great company," "If only operations would execute the training manual the way it's written, then we'd be a great company," "If only the marketing people would build our image in the market-place, then we'd be a great company," and "If only business development would develop more business, then we would be a great company." Yikes. They point the finger of blame at everyone else and trivialize their real organizational issues.

Corporate Correction: "When I improve,..."

A far healthier mindset says, "When I improve as a leader and as a manager, the company will be better off." By turning your focus inward, you can change the one and only person you're capable of changing. You can't make someone be something they don't want to be. Only that person can choose to change how they behave. However, you can change your behaviors. When a group of individuals collectively decides to improve its behaviors, real change happens in an organization. "If only..." wastes your time, talent, and energy. Avoid it and focus instead on what you can do to make the company a more successful organization.

THE CORPORATE CATALYSTIC CONVERTER

☑ Clarify the corporate nonsense.

If it looks like nonsense, sounds like nonsense, and acts like nonsense, it probably is nonsense. My mother always admonishes me to use common sense in every situation. Turns out she's right again. Common sense says to stop doing things that ruin your business.

☑ Another way to clarify corporate nonsense is to look for exceptions to the rule.

For example, if you see three examples that don't support the business maxim, you should start to doubt the validity of it.

☑ Avoid the nonsense.

Once you're reasonably convinced that something is nonsense, do everything you can to get yourself, your group, and your organization to stop doing it. Wasting time on corporate nonsense uses up valuable energy and resources that could be redirected toward more meaningful issues.

Recommended Resources for Corporate Catalysts

The Maverick Mindset: Finding the Courage to Journey from Fear to Freedom by Doug Hall with David Wecker (Simon & Schuster, 1997).

These two authors do a fine job of slicing through a good deal of nonsense and providing the reader with practical suggestions on how to maintain their common sense. While it's geared toward entrepreneurs, it has a lot of applications for employees inside large organizations.

First, Break All the Rules: What the World's Greatest Managers Do Differently by Marcus Buckingham and Curt Coffman (Simon & Schuster, 1999).

These two authors take on many management "truths" and set them on their ears. They dive into real-life organizations and learn what has really worked as opposed to what people thought would work. One thing that intrigued me about this book is the authors took the opposite approach to research than the way I did. While I spent about 2,500 hours on-site observing executives in a variety of business settings and providing more than 900 executive coaching sessions, these two based their book on in-depth interviews of more than 80,000 managers completed by the Gallup Organization.

Chapter 9

CREATIVE CONTRARIAN

YOU'VE STAYED WITH ME THIS FAR, so you probably realize that being a corporate catalyst means you may have to challenge some of the status quo happenings in your organization. This is no small matter. If you push too lightly, nothing changes. If you push in the wrong way, you blow up your relationships with other people, lose your credibility, and nothing changes. If you really want to serve as an effective catalyst, you need to creatively challenge the way people think in a way that drives better results. In other words, you need to be a leader.

Prerequisites for Creative Contrarians

Being a successful contrarian requires something other than shooting down every idea you hear. Here are five important characteristics of effective contrarians:

Strong Self-Esteem

Self-esteem, in a business sense, is the value you believe you can bring to your organization. If your self-esteem is low, you won't ever offer an alternative perspective. You'll simply assume you don't have anything new to offer. There are four ways to strengthen your self-esteem:

- Know and apply your strengths. The more you understand and use your greatest strengths, the more you realize how much value you have to offer to other people in your organization and your customers.

- Recall one of your past success stories. Recall your desired objective, the obstacles you faced, the way you overcame adversity, the lessons you learned and how it felt when you finally achieved that objective. Then clarify how you can apply the lessons from that situation to your current set of circumstances. Recalling past success stories helps you realize the value you bring to the challenges your organization faces today.

- Act with integrity. The more often you do what you believe in, the more you trust yourself, and the higher your self-esteem goes up. When you do what you don't believe is the right thing to do, the more you lose faith in yourself, and the lower your self-esteem goes down.

- See the strengths in other people. The more attention you give to the strengths in other people, the more you see your own strengths. This requires a conscious effort to sidestep the gossiping and backstabbing that happens every day in organizations. When you whine about other people, you subconsciously begin to focus on your own weaknesses. I used to think I could build myself up by tearing other people down. What I found was that I just tore my self-esteem down even faster.

Capacity to Lose Your Job

The idea that you can accelerate your career by being capable of losing your job seems like an oxymoron. However, if you are psychologically capable of losing your job, you are free to challenge your boss and other people. If your esteem rests on maintaining your current label, you won't be an effective contrarian.

Comfortable With Ostracism

If you have to be popular at all times, forget about being a corporate catalyst. That's right, just close the book. Sorry it took me so long to warn you. As a contrarian, you will be both admired and admonished. You will be looked up to and held up as a role model in some situations and ridiculed in other situations. It is very hard work to challenge the overwhelming majority. However, the creative contrarian's goal is not popularity. He or she wants to accelerate the significant, sustainable, and profitable growth of his or her organization.

Master the Fundamentals

You have to walk your talk in terms of your leadership and management approaches. Promoting an approach to another person that you're not willing to try is counterproductive. Your actions will speak louder than your words.

How Not to Push Back

I often hear people say that they pushed back on the status quo mentality and failed miserably to change anything, but then they brag about their actions like they're wearing red badges of courage. *Hello.* The goal is to improve the HPOs, not to be a contrarian. If you didn't cause people to think differently, they won't change their approaches or results. Here are ways *not* to be an effective contrarian:

- Embarrass the other person. Make them look stupid in front of their boss, peers, direct reports, and customers. Not only will they not change, they will spend the remainder of their career searching for opportunities to get back at you.

- Have your guns blazing every day. Push back on every issue at every meeting. Play the devil's advocate on what was served for lunch, why certain bonuses were given out, the group's sales strategy, the size of the facility, and on and on. Be sure to turn over every rock until you've driven everyone in the group insane.

- Whine, whine, and whine some more. Offer no solutions, but just keep complaining about some aspect of your organization and never let up. Instead of offering a logical and coherent perspective to your boss and peer group, just complain behind your boss's back about all of the stupid things happening in your organization.

- Mutter under your breath about the situation. Rather than coming out with an alternative approach, just roll your eyes, shake your head, and mutter semi-intelligent phrases that people around you can hear clearly. Instead of having the courage to speak up, just shoot down the people around you with your arrogant disgust.

- Use sarcasm. Say things such as, "After we implement this new program, we'll fly to the moon for the party," or "I think it's a great idea. I also have some swamp land I want to sell you." These sarcastic remarks may win you some short-term laughter, but it doesn't add much to the mix.

- Act like the long-lost genius. Tell the group exactly what everyone should think and do. At first, you appear to be the knight in shining armor who rode in to save the group. Unfortunately, the more you push your solution onto other people, the more they will push back to prove you're wrong.

- Be extremely long-winded. Sit in a 90-minute meeting with 20 other people and go on for 15 minutes expounding on your perspective. It just wears other people down and keeps them from responding. They'll do anything, including staying quiet, for you to shut up.

- Offer unsolicited advice. Lean over at a crowded luncheon table and tell somebody sitting two seats away why they've approached the situation in the wrong way and what they should do differently.

Case Study: The Three Contrarians

I could call this case study "The 500 Contrarians" because virtually every super-successful person was a contrarian at some point in his career. When Warren Buffett openly admitted he did not buy technology stocks in the late 1990s, everyone thought the investing industry had passed him by. Then, three years later, when his investments soared and others plummeted, people realized he was the intelligent contrarian. Jack Welch was not promoted a few times and almost left GE at least once because of his contrarian approach to the then conservative GE culture. As CEO, he threw virtually every aspect of GE's approach to business out the window and crafted a new approach built on relentless improvement in terms of both people and processes. He also encouraged Jeffrey Immelt, his successor as CEO, to be just as much of a contrarian. Oprah Winfrey focused on promoting books and interviewing quality guests as her competitors chased the bizarre and deviant characters in society. In the end, either you serve as a creative contrarian or you probably don't take your organization to the next level. It's never enough to just do your job and stay out of trouble.

How to Challenge Effectively

How can a person challenge the status quo in a way that other people hear their alternative perspective, respect it, consider it, and possibly change their behaviors? Here are some suggestions:

➢ **Think before you communicate.**

Jot down your contrarian statement and read it over a few times before you say it. Most ineffective contrarians lose their impact because they get overly emotional at the moment of delivery. Keep your content, but phrase it in a way that people can consider it.

➢ **Replay what you just heard.**

If you hear an outrageous statement, repeat it so everyone can hear it. Ask if that was what the person meant to say. For example, you could say, "I just heard you say you want us to grow our comp sales from 3 percent to 21 percent over the next 12 months. Is that right?" If the other person affirms it, you could say, "That's 700 percent growth in one year. Does that seem realistic to you?"

➢ **Use self-deprecating humor.**

If your group wants to fire a couple of new employees for mistakes they made, you might say, "If my bosses had fired me for every mistake I made in the first year, I'd be out on the streets right now. Let's give them another chance to learn."

➢ **Be dramatic.**

If you're rational 99 percent of the time, an occasional outburst can be effective. Stand up at a meeting where your project is about to get cut and say, "Look, we didn't just work 10 months to throw this project away. We want to find an answer, and we *will* find an answer. Give us 30 days to prove success is right in front of us."

➢ **Demonstrate visual disconnects.**

For example, show a videotape of a customer being treated rudely under a banner that says, "Our Customers Are the Business." It brings to reality the lack of genuineness in the corporate mission statement.

➢ **Provide examples of verbal disconnects.**

Repeat two statements that don't match. In April 2003, Don Carty, then the CEO of American Airlines, told pilots and flight attendants to take pay cuts for the good of the team while telling executives their incomes were secure no matter what happened. A creative contrarian would have pushed him back before he spoke to the union members.

➢ **Know the facts and base your input on the facts.**

If you say your organization provides horrible customer service, provide specific examples and statistics of poor customer service. Let the facts and logic make your case and stir the emotions in the room.

➢ **Use low frequency.**

Select your opportunities to be a contrarian very carefully. If you argue too often, no one will listen to you. They will tune you out. If you raise your hand and challenge the status quo 5 to 10 percent of the time, people listen. Also, be prepared to propose a different solution in an efficient manner.

➢ **Focus on HPOs.**

Save your contrarian point of view for the really important outcomes. If you try to improve every single outcome in your company, you get lost in the quicksand of being tuned out long before the really important stuff comes up.

➢ **Meet multiple personality needs.**

You haven't really impacted the way other people think if you only met the personality needs of one type of decision-maker. If you only met the needs of the conscientious person, the quick decision-maker and emotional decision-maker may both feel left out. That makes you only partly effective in terms of effecting sustainable change in your organization.

➢ **Create a real sense of danger.**

If people don't feel the organization's results are threatened by remaining status quo, it will be tough to get them to change. Why should they change if things are going so well right now? Unless they see the impending danger, they may not adjust at all.

➢ **Clarify the golden opportunity.**

This is the opposite approach to the previous one. Make sure people realize the extraordinary upside of changing their behaviors. If they perceive the potential good far outweighs the potential bad, they may change their behaviors.

➢ **Focus on the rational self-interests of each group you attempt to affect.**

Before you say anything or do anything, take the time to understand why they would consider changing. Once you understand their perspectives, explain your alternative approach in a step-by-step manner that connects to the rational self-interests of different people in the room. Get people nodding their heads and saying, "That sounds good to me."

➢ **Reverse the risks.**

You have a small chance of getting people to change their behaviors if you put all of the risks on their shoulders. For example, telling people they need to spend more time on quality control isn't likely to go very far if you continue to base their incentive program on increasing transactions. However, if you tell employees they need to shift to a long-term customer focus from short-term transactional selling and you create an incentive program that rewards fewer product returns, you have a better chance to succeed. John Paul Jones, a naval captain and a founder of the U.S. Navy, achieved legendary status by reversing risks. On September 23, 1779, his ship, *Bon Homme Richard*, was blasted in the initial exchange with the enemy ship, *HMS Sherapis*. When the enemy captain, Richard Pearson, asked him if he wanted to surrender, John Paul Jones said, "I have not yet begun to fight!" He then led his crew to abandon their sinking ship and literally climb aboard and take over the enemy's ship. He reversed the risk of losing his ship by converting it into the transformational event that led to victory. How can you reverse the risks your organization faces today? Do you need to abandon a current strategy, take on a competitor's strategy, and execute it better than they do? Challenge your team members to realize they have not yet begun to fight.

Case Study: Revolutionaries Old and New

In the April 13, 2004 issue of the *Wall Street Journal*, Dr. William Hunter said one of his professors told him the difference between a good scientist and a great scientist is the quality of the questions posed. Dr. Hunter, CEO of Angiotech Pharmaceuticals, partnered with the Boston Scientific Corporation to develop a pioneering coronary stent named TAXUS, which is coated with the cancer drug paclitaxel. He served as a creative contrarian by challenging the traditional scientific approach of keeping pharmaceuticals separate from medical devices. Rather than following the traditional path of trying to make better stents, Hunter stepped in with an altogether different question when he asked, "What does the body do to those stents and why do those stents fail?" By asking that question, he caused the group to think differently and ultimately to combine the traditional stents with the drug coating. This revolutionized the medical approach to dealing with the growth of scar tissue after surgery. Dr. Hunter provided a classic example of how effective leadership generates powerful innovations within the core purpose of a business. The two founders of Boston Scientific Corporation, John Abele and Pete Nicholas, met while watching their children play grade school soccer in the late 1970s.

They decided to create a business that would develop innovative and less invasive medical tools. The company never lost its direction, and more than 25 years later, Dr. Hunter provided the leadership that helped to produce the innovative new tool that nearly doubled the company's revenues.

Alexander Hamilton may have been the original American corporate catalyst, except the "corporation" he sought to improve was the fledgling United States of America. Ron Chernow, in his book *Alexander Hamilton* (Penquin Books, 2004), explained how Hamilton successfully served as a contrarian regarding paying off the U.S. government's $54 million in national debt and $25 million in state debts. Many patriots doubted the prospects of ever getting their money back and, consequently, accepted 15 cents on the dollar for their IOUs from speculators. When Hamilton argued the government had to eventually pay off its debt, he also drove home the point that the money must be paid to the speculators and not to the patriots who served in the U.S. military to forge the new nation. Hamilton's rationale was "securities are freely transferable and that buyers should assume the right of profit or loss from their transactions." Because he stuck to his vastly unpopular stance, he put in motion a great deal of the long-term basis for securities trading in the United States.

Corporate Catalyst Tip #9:
See the Value of Being a Contrarian

Of course, the first person you need to sell on the value of being a contrarian is you. If you don't see the short- and long-term benefit of challenging current approaches and offering alternative solutions, you'll never do it. It's uncomfortable to be the contrarian. It's hard to be an effective contrarian. In order to do it, you need to believe being a contrarian will improve your organization, your group, and your career. You may lose your job, but corporate catalysts would rather have the income security that goes to the creative contrarian than the theoretical job security that goes to the status quoer.

THE CORPORATE CATALYSTIC CONVERTER

☑ Self-esteem is the currency for effective contrarians.

Unless you clearly understand the value you bring to a situation, you probably won't challenge the mindset of the group.

☑ The creative contrarian understands that what most people consider a career risk is actually a very wise gamble.

Because so few people ever push back their boss or question the current approach, the ones who *do* easily stand out in the crowd. If that leads to losing your job, so be it. Getting fired might accelerate your ability to get to an organization where you will be taken more seriously.

☑ Remember that getting fired or demoted just for the sake of getting fired or demoted is not a noble act.

The creative contrarian realizes that embarrassing other people or dictating orders is at best a short-term thrill and at worst destroys his credibility for the long term.

☑ The effective contrarian represents a true social artist because he or she gets people to consider opposing points of view without dismissing them.

This requires patience, flexibility, and an array of effective intervention techniques.

Recommended Resources for Corporate Catalysts

Warren Buffett Speaks: Wit and Wisdom From the World's Greatest Investor by Janet Lowe (John Wiley & Sons, 1997).

Warren Buffett walks to the beat of his own drum and doesn't mind sharing his opinions with anybody on virtually anything. On the one hand, he's a famously conservative investor, and on the other hand, he does and says things that run significantly contrary to traditional ways. He uses analogies as a brilliant way to challenge other people's thinking.

How to Win Friends & Influence People by Dale Carnegie (Simon & Schuster, 1936).

This true classic explains how to oppose other people in a way they can consider your point of view. At first, advice such as "never condemn, criticize, or complain," may seem like a very, very passive approach to challenging the status quo, but it actually provides an excellent parameter for deciding how to intervene. Criticizing someone rarely gets him to rethink his approach to business, but asking an open-ended question or sharing an analogous situation may work.

Execution: The Discipline of Getting Things Done by Larry Bossidy and Ram Charan (Crown Business, 2002).

This may seem like an odd choice for a chapter on being a contrarian because the authors write about the building blocks, the fundamentals, of a successful business. However, when you consider the amount of books on the "new economy," silver bullet approaches and management fads, these two authors stand out as modern contrarians by essentially saying, "Let's go back to the basics."

Chapter 10

CORPORATE CATALYSTS CONCLUSIONS AND SELF-ASSESSMENT TOOL

A CORPORATE CATALYST IS A RARITY IN ANY ORGANIZATION. He is the person who lifts the organization to the next level. His work integrates a variety of skills that deliver a positive impact to the significant, sustainable, and profitable growth of his or her business.

12 Conclusions About Corporate Catalysts

1. Benefits are both intangible and real.

Influencing others, organizing resources, clarifying desired outcomes, and holding people accountable happen behind the scenes. No glory comes with doing the endless details required of corporate catalysts. However, real results are generated, reputations are enhanced, and greater career opportunities do open up. Take time to clarify the reasons why you want to serve as a corporate catalyst. Understand you can make a meaningful difference in the lives of other people and in the history of your organization. Realize you enhance your skills for future challenges. The benefits are not instantaneous, visible, or obvious, but they are long-term and significant.

2.   Understand your value.

In *Merriam-Webster's Dictionary*, a catalyst is "a person or thing acting as the stimulus in bringing about something." The first step in order for you to be a catalyst in your organization is to realize what value you bring to the party. By understanding and applying your strengths, you can serve as the stimulus that brings about better and more sustainable business results.

3.   Avoid fallacy investments.

Throughout this book, multiple fallacies have been highlighted and attacked. I encourage you to identify corporate fallacies and eliminate them. Stop wasting your time on them. Rather than saying, "We do so many stupid things around here," and then continuing to do them, be the one who pushes back and challenges the faulty thought process.

4.   Understand outcomes and others.

The corporate catalyst keeps two entities in mind at all times: the desired business outcomes and the people who generate those outcomes. A strategy is not effective if it can't be executed. That sounds obvious, and yet sometimes what seems obvious in the meeting room does not mesh with the reality of executing it. Work to influence and manage effectively toward delivering better results, which requires understanding the strengths of your group and the progress required to achieve the desired outcome.

5.   "Good things come to those who wait."

This is one of my dad's favorite sayings. I hated hearing it when I was 17 and he would only let me drive the family car once a month. I hated it when he made me keep my money in the bank for college and didn't allow me to buy my own car. Now, at 41, I see his wisdom. The companies that focus on the long term and execute in the short term are the really big winners. Rather than focusing solely on improving your quarterly earnings per share or short-term results, focus on improving the long-term result of significant, sustainable, and profitable growth.

6.   Framework and freedom.

Effective managers provide a balance between structure and independence. They clarify the Playing Field and stay out of the way. They define what is expected in terms of results and behaviors, and they let their employees perform autonomously every day. This creates the environment where motivated people excel.

7.   Add assistance, apply accountability.

Effective managers serve as coaches by asking questions, listening to ideas, offering suggestions, and collaborating with their direct reports to generate even better approaches to the business. They also serve as standard-bearers by holding their direct reports accountable for delivering results and behaving in accordance with the stated values.

8.   Innovation is not the endgame, it's the everyday game.

It's not enough to develop innovative products and services for your customers. That is only effective if the customers believe they gain more value from these new products and services, they are willing to pay for them, and you have the capacity to distribute them efficiently. This is why cross-functional teamwork is critically important. Pull together key members from operations, marketing, purchasing, distribution, finance, and human resources in the early stages of developing innovative products and services. Their job is to collectively improve the critical business outcomes for your organization. Innovation is required for success, but does not constitute success.

9.   Synergy and serendipity.

Synergy is what happens when all your products and services promote and support all your other products and services, and they all fit under the umbrella of a common concept. This is how you build a brand. A brand is the perception of value customers think they get from your organization or prospects think they would get if they bought from your organization. The more value people perceive, the more you retain your customers and attract new ones. Serendipity refers to being open to new possibilities and opportunities. As your brand gets stronger, new opportunities come your way on a regular basis. Be open to them. You don't know who will open another door for you or how big the room will be. The corporate catalyst helps members of his or her group see the long-term value of synergy and serendipity.

10.   The 10-year hiring rule.

If you knew your organization had to keep the person you're hiring for at least 10 years, would you still hire the person? Why or why not?

By answering those questions, you quickly see what underlies your hiring decision. If you want to build a great organization for the long term, hire people you want for the long term.

11. Relationship currency.

A business is nothing more than the exchange of value. You create value, sell it, and get value in return. The only way to know what is of value to other people is to understand those people. Consequently, relationship currency is the most important currency in all of business. Invest time and energy into better understanding your customers and your colleagues at work. Find out their desired outcomes. Work to add value to them and help them achieve their desired outcomes. In other words, build value-added relationships.

Don't Use Your Gifts Lightly

Being a corporate catalyst is a privilege and a responsibility. Having the capacity to effectively influence people, intelligently manage resources, and courageously challenge the status quo provides you with an extraordinary means for making a positive difference. Apply these gifts toward improving your organization's most meaningful outcomes. Don't waste your time, talent, or energy on trivial things. A corporate catalyst has the ability to make an extraordinary difference and the responsibility to apply his or her gifts where they matter the most.

12. Push 'em back, push 'em back, way back.

If you are going to accelerate an organization, you probably have to challenge some aspect of the current situation. That makes some people very uncomfortable. Get used to it because it never goes away.

The Corporate Catalyst Self-Assessment Tool

Circle the letter of the response that most closely resembles your situation.

1. How do you use the defined purpose of your business to guide decision-making?

    A. I post the purpose of our business in our lobby area.

    B. In our annual business meeting, I discuss the purpose of our business and use it as a filter in our annual strategic planning.

    C. At the bottom of every meeting agenda, I put this question: "Will these activities support the defined purpose of our business, which is ____." Our group then puts every decision through that filter and eliminates the ones that don't fit.

2. How do you ensure your highest priority outcomes are leading to significant, sustainable, and profitable growth?

    A. I examine our revenues to determine our financial trends.

    B. I set cash flow as a higher priority than revenues.

    C. I have my group look at the activities generating positive cash flow. We determine if they support our defined purpose as a business and if they can become part of our ongoing operations. We work to replace the ones that don't support these two aspects.

3. How do you keep the people in your organization focused on generating long-term success?

    A. At our quarterly staff meetings, I make certain to put "The Value of Long-Term Thinking" on the agenda and discuss it with my group.

    B. In one-on-one sessions, I always ask people what they are doing today to improve the business two years from now.

    C. Our bonus program is 30 percent based on the results our company has generated over the past two years.

4. What do you currently do that is effective in communicating with your work team?

    A. Once a year I send a written communication to each member of my group thanking them for their efforts and reminding them I always welcome their insights.

B. On a quarterly basis I go to lunch with each individual in my group to explore the underlying issues that generate success and failure in our business. Then I work with our group to overcome the negative issues and build on our collective strengths.

C. I meet weekly with at least two members of my group and ask open-ended questions to better understand their objectives, issues, and action plans. I follow up these conversations with written encouragement, suggestions for improving results, and actions I will do to support them.

5. How do you influence other people to improve results for the organization and the individuals in it?

A. I bring my team together once each quarter and provide them with an overview of the business and my suggestions on how we can improve results. I always provide a dinner for the group the night before our meeting.

B. I meet monthly with different members and ask open-ended questions to better understand their perspectives on the organization and the individuals in it. I then provide both verbal and written suggestions to the individual on how they might play a more effective role in improving the organization.

C. I use a variety of approaches to influence the members of my group, ranging from giving speeches to facilitating discussions to empowering individuals to providing one-on-one coaching sessions. I identify each individual's personality needs in different situations and try to communicate in the appropriate manner for each person. I use a mixture of handwritten notes, bullet-point summaries, logical step-by-step explanations, and testimonials to influence people.

6. What do you do to increase the clarity and understanding your team members have of your group's most important objectives?

A. I post the group's goals in a public area for all members of the group to see daily. We update the actual results on a weekly basis.

    B. I have an annual retreat where all members of the group discuss their objectives, strategies, tactics, and metrics for the upcoming year. Each person receives feedback from the other members regarding his or her plan.

    C. On a monthly basis, I discuss with my group members their actual results versus projected results, the activities that have worked well, the ones that have not worked well, the lessons they have learned, and any necessary adjustments for future strategy and tactics.

7. How do you clarify the Playing Field, coach individuals to greater results and more effective behaviors, and hold people accountable?

    A. I send the business plan for our group to each team member and explain how the bonus system is set up based on their results. At mid-year, I go over the plan with each individual, assess his performance based purely on his actual results, and give advice on how to optimize his bonus.

    B. I set aside one day each year to meet with my team to map out their strategies, tactics, and goals for the upcoming year. On a quarterly basis, I meet with my team to evaluate our progress as a group and make adjustments.

    C. I set aside two days each year to discuss with my team the values and strategies our group operates within and the expected short-term and long-term objectives for each of them. I have a monthly discussion with both the entire group and each individual separately to evaluate behaviors and results and to determine any necessary adjustments going forward.

8. What do you do to learn from other companies?

    A. Once a year I put together a cross-functional group to study and benchmark another company. They search for practices we could apply in our business.

    B. I read the *Wall Street Journal* each day as well as *BusinessWeek* and *Fortune* magazine. This provides me with an overview of what is happening on an ongoing basis.

C. Once a quarter we bring together department heads to discuss the lessons they have learned from companies outside of our industry. Then we look for ways to apply these ideas within the framework of the purpose of our business.

9. What do the members of your group currently do to build on each other's ideas?

A. Group members work independently and compare finished proposals as time permits.

B. Group members meet at organized weekly sessions and use an agenda to track progress and compare notes.

C. Group members meet spontaneously on a daily basis to exchange ideas on key projects and look for ways to combine ideas into even better ideas.

10. How does your group increase the value customers receive?

A. Each year our team discusses what changes need to be made to our products/services that would add more value to our customers.

B. We survey 20 customers each quarter and identify what we do that adds real value, adds no value, or has an adverse affect on them. We consider this input and make adjustments where we feel it is appropriate.

C. Every month we interview at least a dozen customers to understand how our products/services add value to them and how they could be improved to add even more value. We then examine what we currently do and make adjustments to add more value. We then track our changes with our customers to determine whether or not these changes were effective for them.

11. How does your group enhance the perception of value your customers and prospects have regarding your organization?

A. Once a year we bring in branding experts to facilitate a session on how to build a more successful brand.

B. Every six months our team members attend a half-day meeting to discuss our brand and what they think can be done to improve it.

C. Each quarter we interview a dozen customers and ask them what they perceive to be the value they receive from our organization. We also ask a dozen people who have heard of our organization, but never bought from us, what they perceive to be the potential value they could gain from our organization. We then establish and execute a 90-day action plan for better positioning the value we offer.

12. What do you do that adds value to the members of your group?

A. Once a quarter I look for a book to recommend to all the members of my group that is relevant to the project we're working on.

B. Each month I identify at least one best practice a competitor uses to drive results and highlight this best practice for my group to consider for future application.

C. I work to understand the strengths and passions of each member. Each week I give at least one person a suggestion, an open-ended question, or an article on how he can leverage his strengths or passions to drive even better results for our organization.

13. How do you apply your greatest strengths and passions toward improving your most important professional objectives?

A. Every year I schedule a two-day learning experience around my area of passion and identify two ways I can implement what I've learned.

B. Each quarter I set aside a day to enhance my skills in my areas of interest, and I share my findings with my colleagues and direct reports.

C. On a weekly basis, I read and study the latest findings in my areas of passion and actively look to apply what I've learned toward my most important objectives at work.

14. What do you currently do to broaden your perspective?

A. I read a book outside of my area of expertise every year to broaden my understanding of business issues.

   B. Each quarter I spend a day working in a different depart-
      ment to better understand the issues my colleagues deal
      with on a regular basis.
   C. Every day I read a newspaper or magazine to broaden
      my understanding of general business trends.

15. What do you do to challenge the ineffective status quo activities
    in your organization?

   A. When I disagree with something I hear at a meeting, I
      raise my hand and let everyone know why I don't think
      the idea is good for our company.
   B. When I disagree with something I hear at a meeting, I
      give myself 24 hours to think through my response, put
      my rationale for not doing the idea in writing, and offer
      three alternative approaches for the group to consider.
   C. When I disagree with something, I do the research nec-
      essary to determine if there is factual evidence support-
      ing my opposition to the idea. I then present my point of
      view with the facts in a clear and rational manner. I fol-
      low this up with at least three alternatives I consider to
      be better approaches and my rationale for each of them.

16. How do you build stronger business relationships both inside
    and outside your organization?

   A. I put a lot of emphasis on really listening to other people,
      letting go of everything going on around me and being
      fully present for the other person.
   B. I identify 25 people who are critical to the success of my
      business. I stay in touch with each of them a minimum of
      once a month via a live conversation, a handwritten note,
      or a personal e-mail.
   C. Every month I add value to each of my top 25 people
      through sending them a relevant article or book, intro-
      ducing them to other people who might enhance their
      results, offering timely information that can accelerate
      their career, asking questions to help them break through
      their current obstacles, or offering assistance on a major
      objective they are working toward.

17. How do the members of your group decide what to do and what to stop doing in order to improve results in your organization's highest priority outcomes?

   A. On a semiannual basis, I meet with each individual in my group to assess his or her performance.

   B. Every quarter I meet with each member of my group to review all of the activities he or she has done to improve high priority results. We work to hone the list to the fewest tactics that will have the greatest positive impact on achieving the desired outcomes.

   C. On a weekly basis, I meet with all members of my group to discuss their activities and identify which ones enhance their progress toward the desired outcomes, which ones have no effect on results, and which ones have an adverse effect. We then select the activities to continue, the ones to stop, and the new ones to start.

18. How do you maintain consistency within your brand?

   A. At our annual planning session, we go through our proposed strategy and tactics and ask ourselves if they support the perception of value for which we want to be known.

   B. After each initiative, we evaluate whether the project strengthened or weakened our desired brand, regardless of how much revenue it generated.

   C. Before a new initiative is implemented, we have representatives of marketing, operations, human resources, finance, and purchasing discuss whether they believe the project supports or hurts the desired brand. Each person lays out his or her rationale and offers suggestions on how to leverage the new project to enhance our brand.

19. How do you increase your chances of hiring the right people for your organization?

   A. We attempt to have the candidate attend a variety of our internal functions before we make a permanent offer to them.

   B. Every candidate for every position must be interviewed by at least four people inside our group, and they must receive at least two votes to hire them before they can come on board.

C. We make a list of interview questions, role plays, and case studies to better understand if the candidate has the desired values, passions, and talent. We use these as a template for interviewing the candidate. Each candidate is interviewed by a minimum of four people. These people have an open discussion about the candidate. At least three people have to give a vote of confidence to hire them.

20. How do you avoid investing time, energy, and money into "corporate nonsense"?

A. Once a year we hold a "nonsense discussion" for all of the group members. Each person has the opportunity to argue that some commonly held belief is really non-sensical. The group discusses whether to eliminate that perspective in their decision-making progress.

B. We use an ongoing "Nonsense Box." Any employee can drop a note into the box at any time to discuss the valid-ity of a policy, strategy, or decision. Once a quarter our group examines these comments and decides what to do and how to respond.

C. Each quarter, we have an open forum to discuss our busi-ness with all members of our group and extended groups. One common agenda item is "Taking Out the Corporate Nonsense." Anyone can challenge any belief that guides the organization. A person can do it anonymously if he or she prefers. Each statement is discussed and alterna-tives are examined.

Scoring: A = 1 point, B = 3 points, C = 5 points

85–100 Points = Accelerator

You are a corporate catalyst. You raise the bar for your organiza-tion and help to generate sustainable and profitable growth. However, the key to your future success is the same as the key to your past suc-cess: continual daily improvement! Keep striving to be more effective.

71–84 Points = Strong Performer

You are a strong performer. You improve at the same rate year after year. Your organization knows it can count on you to steadily improve results. However, your improvement is predictable. You're not pushing the envelope on a daily basis as much as you can. You're not accelerating, but merely steadily improving over the course of a year.

55–69 Points = Status Quoer

You're essentially providing the same performance you did five years ago. While it's true your organization knows what it will get from you, it also realizes your impact will not be greater or less than it has always been. You need to shake up your thinking, invest the necessary time and energy to reflect on what is working and on what is not working, and strive to move beyond "what has always worked in the past."

Below 55 Points = Decliner

You're acting as though your best days are behind you. You're letting your performance slip on a continuous basis. You're gradually falling into a mode of "punching the clock and picking up a check." Your work has become merely a job. It's time for you to take a day off and determine what you want your future to look like.

General Suggestions

- Don't compare your score to other people. It's a waste of time. The goal is to always improve your own performance.
- Add up your points and search for ways to improve your overall score.
- Look at each question and determine what you want to do to enhance your impact.
- Find one area where you scored a 5 and search for ways to improve your performance.
- Find one area where you scored a 1 and search for ways to improve your performance.
- Ask your colleagues and customers for feedback on each of these areas.

♦ Create your own assessment tool and work to consistently raise your score.

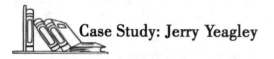 ## Case Study: Jerry Yeagley

This is a bit of an unusual case study to end with, but I think Jerry Yeagley is a perfect example of a corporate catalyst. He served as the head soccer coach at Indiana University from 1963 to 2003. For the first 10 years, he was in charge of the club soccer team and kept hoping it would gain varsity status.

In the early days, he took the long-term view of what the program could become rather than focusing on what it was not. In some ways, a state university is like a large corporation, and a soccer program is like a single department. Just as in a corporation, it can take a very long time for your department to gain critical support. Yeagley persevered, maintained his classy composure, and continued to seek support. In 1973, 10 years after he came to IU, the club soccer team gained varsity status.

Coach Yeagley then provided both effective leadership and management in guiding the program to six NCAA Division I national championships. His keys to success represent everything in this book. He communicated as effectively with the superstars as he did with the non-scholarship players who walked on to the team. He displayed extraordinary attention to detail. He influenced university administrators, high school players, college stars, and assistant coaches extremely well. He was just as good at organizing resources and holding people accountable as he was at influencing the way people thought.

Jerry Yeagley didn't even become a varsity coach until his 11th year, but he went on to become the winningest coach in NCAA Division I soccer history. At his retirement banquet, he passed the credit on to his players, his assistants, and the university administrators. He said the core of the reason for his success was "The Indiana University Soccer Player." He defined this person as having four qualities: inspired through personal motivation, a positive attitude, integrity, and pride in their uniform. He said the IU Soccer Player always strives to improve.

His goal was never to win soccer games, but rather for his teams to achieve excellence. In the beginning, the university didn't want a varsity soccer team. In the end, the university gained a great deal of positive public relations because it had the most successful soccer program in the country. This is the kind of impact you can have in your organization.

Corporate Catalyst Tip #10:
Pursue Progress, Not Perfection

Perfection is an illusion, and pursuing it is dysfunctional. The corporate catalyst pursues progress, not perfection. Corporate catalysts know their capacities to add more value and generate greater opportunities is based on continually improving. They never set leadership or management goals to reach, but always set the goal to reach forward as a leader and a manager. They know the ultimate secret to being a corporate catalyst is very simple: *be better today than you were yesterday, be better tomorrow than you are today, and do that day after day.*

Recommended Resources for Corporate Catalysts

Profitable Growth Is Everyone's Business: 10 Tools You Can Use Monday Morning by Ram Charan (Crown Business, 2004).

I close with this book recommendation because I believe Charan and I walk to the beat of the same drummer: keep the advice practical; base your research on real-life observed behavior; and focus on generating significant, sustainable, and profitable growth.

Index

About the Author

As a consultant and professional speaker, **Dan Coughlin** works with executives and entrepreneurs to accelerate their critical business outcomes. His clients include McDonald's Corporation, The Coca-Cola Company, Marriott International, Citigroup, Eli Lilly & Sons, SBC Communications, IKON Office Solutions, Salomon Smith Barney, McCarthy Building Companies, Fru-Con Construction, Massachusetts Bar Leadership Institute, St. Louis Cardinals, ONDEO-Nalco Corporation, Heartland Dental Care, Auxeris Therapeutics, Cassens Transport, Brown Shoe Company, Ritter's Frozen Custard, Four Seasons Group, GSD&M, the American Bar Association, and more than 70 other organizations.

Dan has provided in excess of 400 interactive presentations in more than 30 states on leadership, management, teamwork, branding, strategy and innovation. As an Executive Coach, he has provided more than 900 individual Executive Coaching sessions for presidents, vice presidents, and senior directors of Fortune 500 companies and major privately owned firms.

Dan frequently contributes articles to trade journals on how to accelerate critical business outcomes. He holds a bachelor's of science degree in mechanical engineering from the University of Notre Dame and a master's degree in arts and teaching from Webster University. A former NCAA Division I head coach for DePaul University, Dan has served as president for the National Speakers Association St. Louis Chapter, Institute of Management Consultants St. Louis Chapter, and Notre Dame Club of St. Louis. He has taught courses on entrepreneurship and managerial leadership for St. Louis University and Webster University's Graduate School of Business.

Dan has more than 100 free articles on how to accelerate the achievement of your highest priority business outcomes on his Website, *www.thecoughlincompany.com*. At the Website, you can also sign up for his free monthly electronic newsletter, *Corporate & Career Catalyst*.

Dan lives in St. Louis, Missouri, with his wife, Barb, and their children, Sarah and Ben.